How The Holy Spirit Works

How The
Holy Spirit
Works

JIMMY SWAGGART

Jimmy Swaggart Ministries
P.O. Box 262550 | Baton Rouge, Louisiana 70826-2550
www.jsm.org

ISBN 978-1-941403-58-7

09-163 | COPYRIGHT © 2018 Jimmy Swaggart Ministries®

18 19 20 21 22 23 24 25 26 27 / TS / 10 9 8 7 6 5 4 3 2 1

TABLE OF CONTENTS

INTRODUCTION 1

CHAPTER 1   THE WORD OF THE LORD 7

CHAPTER 2   NO CONDEMNATION .23

CHAPTER 3   THE FLESH AND THE SPIRIT 59

CHAPTER 4   THE BODY AND THE SPIRIT 87

CHAPTER 5   SPIRIT OF ADOPTION 117

CHAPTER 6   HOPE 151

CHAPTER 7   SALVATION 197

CHAPTER 8   THE MIND OF THE SPIRIT 229

CHAPTER 9   THE CALLED 251

CHAPTER 10 PREDESTINATION 275

CHAPTER 11 THE LOVE OF CHRIST 307

How The Holy Spirit Works

INTRODUCTION

INTRODUCTION

WERE YOU TO ASK most any Christian as to how the Holy Spirit works, you would be met with a blank stare. In fact, he or she would not know what you were talking about. That means most Christians simply do not know how the Holy Spirit works, which means that their experience with Him is what one might call a hit-and-miss situation.

As a believer, it is imperative that you know how the Holy Spirit works—what He does and how He does it. Of the three members of the Godhead, the Holy Spirit is the one with whom we do business, so to speak.

To be sure, He most definitely will work for us and with us to a much greater extent if we learn a few things about Him, and above all, how He works within our hearts and lives.

REVELATION

The Lord gave me the answer to this question by revelation. It was most remarkable. And that which He gave to me is what I hope to relate to you in this volume. To be sure, it didn't come quickly, and it didn't come easily, but thank the Lord it did come.

I need His help every day of my life and every hour during the day. So do you. I would pray that this volume will give you the answers to some questions, and above all that you will see a great increase of the working and moving of the Holy Spirit within your heart and life, that is, if you believe that which we will relate to you.

It's not at all difficult to get a believer to believe something wrong. Now that sounds like an oxymoron doesn't it? In reality it is, but it happens to be the truth. Sometimes it's difficult to get Christians to accept that which is truly of the Lord.

I have found out that if I will ask the Lord to lead me in the direction that I ought to go, and help me not to believe that which is false—that's a prayer He will answer, and that's a prayer every believer ought to periodically pray.

As well, I would strongly desire that the Lord would help me to receive this to my heart—relating to Him often that which is right, this which is Scriptural—and to function accordingly. Once again, the Lord will answer that prayer.

As you go through this volume, I would pray it would be with a prayer in your heart—that the Lord would open to you the many truths contained therein. Once again, this is something He will do. If I am able to help you recognize the moving and operation of the Holy Spirit and the working of the Holy Spirit within hearts and lives—especially your own—then our labor in putting this volume together will have been well worth the effort. Thank you for being interested enough to see for yourself.

I'm rejoicing night and day,
As I found the pilgrim way,
For the hand of God in all my life I see.
And the reason for my bliss,
Yes, the secret all is this:
That the Comforter abides with me.

Once my heart was full of sin,
Once I had no peace within,
Till I heard how Jesus died upon the tree.
Then I fell down at His feet,
And there came a peace so sweet,
Now the Comforter abides with me.

He is with me everywhere,
And He knows my every care,
I'm as happy as a bird and just as free.
For the Spirit has control,
Jesus satisfies my soul,
Since the Comforter abides with me.

There's no thirsting for the things
Of the world—they've taken wings,
Long ago I gave them up, and instantly
All my night was turned to day,
All my burdens rolled away,
Now the Comforter abides with me.

He abides, He abides,
Hallelujah He abides with me!
I'm rejoicing night and day
As I walk the narrow way,
For the Comforter abides with me.

How The Holy Spirit Works

THE WORD OF THE LORD

THE WORD OF THE LORD

"THIS ONLY WOULD I learn of you, Did you receive the Spirit by the works of the law, or by the hearing of faith? Are you so foolish? Having begun in the Spirit, are you now made perfect by the flesh?" (Gal. 3:2-3).

If I remember correctly, it was a beautiful spring day sometime in March 1988. It was a Monday.

In those days Frances and I generally stayed home on Mondays, meaning that we did not go into the office at all. I would spend the day in prayer and study of the Word, which I was to do this particular day. Something was to happen that would make this one of the greatest days of my life, but not without the efforts of Satan to hinder, and to hinder greatly.

THE POWERS OF DARKNESS

As I began to seek the Lord that day, I had gone to the backside of our property. Our house and Donnie's house sit on 20 acres of land that is outside the city limits of Baton Rouge. Oftentimes I would walk around the parameters praying, which I did that day. I happened to be at the very backside of the property. At a certain point in time, the powers of darkness began to come against me with a powerful force. In fact, it was about as strong as I had ever experienced such. It was so bad that I remonstrated to the Lord, "You said that You would not put anything on us any harder than we could bear, but with every temptation You would make a way of escape." I then said, "Lord, I think You are allowing Satan too much latitude. No human being can stand this."

I won't go into any detail as to what this was all about, but most Spirit-filled believers know exactly what I'm talking about.

It was like there was a hundred-pound weight on my back and everything dark. Satan's taunts were constant and carried with them a feeling of total helplessness.

I think that Satan, most of the time, has some idea as to what the Lord is going to do with us or for us. Consequently, he tries to hinder, and does so with great power.

THE POWER OF GOD

My complaint to the Lord had not left my mouth when all of a sudden the Holy Spirit, in a powerful way—much more powerful than that of the Evil One—moved upon my heart. One moment it was as if a hundred-pound weight were on my back, and the next moment, I seemed to be floating without a particular problem in the world.

Then the Lord spoke to me. He said, "I am going to show you some things about the Holy Spirit that you do not now know."

That was it—short, sweet, and to the point. What did He mean?

The first thought that came to my mind was this: the Holy Spirit is God. Consequently, there are all kinds of things about Him that I do not know, but somehow I knew that what the Lord was talking about was related to the reason for the powerful opposition by Satan.

There is absolutely nothing like the power of God. One moment the believer staggers under a weight of problems, and the next moment, as the presence of God fills the heart, there is not a problem in the world. There is a peace that accompanies such that words cannot describe. I've never taken a drink of any kind of alcohol in my life. I've never taken any drugs, so I don't know what those things do to you. But I do know this: Even though I've only experienced one side of this equation, and I speak of the side of the Lord, I personally believe there is absolutely nothing that can compare with the presence of God.

WHAT DID THE LORD MEAN?

I had seen the Holy Spirit move upon my heart and life to help me see literally hundreds of thousands of souls brought to a saving knowledge of Jesus Christ, and I am not exaggerating. As well, I had seen tens of thousands, over a period of time, baptized with the mighty Holy Spirit. I knew some things about the Holy Spirit, so what was the Lord talking about?

About that time, Frances called to me at the backdoor stating that there was a phone call, so I hurriedly went to the house to take it.

The brother on the phone was the pastor of one of the largest Southern Baptist churches in the nation. I had met him a few times, but did not really know him that well. However, I so much appreciated him taking the time to call.

At any rate, when I picked up the phone with him on the line, I shouted loudly, "Hallelujah!" (I've often wondered what this dear brother thought about me after our call ended.)

"How are you?" He asked. "How things are going?"

There was no way that I could tell him what had just transpired in my life, but at any rate, I was so grateful for his call.

The Lord did not say to me as to when He would give me this great truth concerning the Holy Spirit. Little did I realize that it would be some nine years before He revealed to me that which He promised that day in 1988.

TIME

At a point in time, when I really saw nothing take place that I felt was the answer as to what the Lord had promised, I asked Him, "Why is it taking so long?"

Several weeks later, at one of the nightly prayer meetings, the Lord answered my prayer, at least to why it was taking so long. He said, *"Precept must be upon precept, precept upon precept; line upon line, line upon line; here a little, and there a little"* (Isa. 28:10).

I knew beyond a shadow of a doubt that the Lord was giving me an answer to my question as to why it was taking so long, but I did not understand at all that which He gave me. What did He mean by this particular Scripture?

Actually, I did not learn what He meant until the Holy Spirit gave me the meaning of the Cross of Christ as it regards the new covenant. In other words, everything had to be in place regarding the Word of God. Nothing could be out of kilter; it had to be straight. When that had taken place—mostly information imparted to me by the Holy Spirit—then the Lord opened the door, thereby keeping His promise that He had made to me, showing me, in a word, how the Holy Spirit works—that which I did not know.

PRECEPT UPON PRECEPT

That which He gave me, which I hope to relate to you, was most definitely known and understood by the apostle Paul, and no doubt many others at that period of the church as well. But from the time of the early church until this present time, I'm not so sure this great truth had been revealed to anyone. Of course I'm only surmising since I cannot know all the things the Lord has done, but what experience I do have tells me that this which He gave me was not something known among believers.

To be frank, I think that which I will relate to you—which will be the epitome of simplicity—will round out the gospel, if you'll think about it a moment.

I think that there are many Christians—and I mean good Christians who love the Lord—who know in their heart of hearts that something is missing. I believe that the Message of the Cross and the way the Holy Spirit works will fill in those blank spots. I know it has for me, and from the testimonies we are receiving, I know it is taking that tact with others as well.

THE MESSAGE OF THE CROSS

That which the Lord gave me in 1997 came in three stages:
1. An understanding of the sin nature.
2. The solution to the sin nature, which is the Cross of Christ.
3. How the Holy Spirit works.

That particular day in 1997 started out like any other day. I went to the office, as was my custom, quite a time before daylight. I was studying the great sixth chapter of Romans. I picked up a book by a noted Greek scholar, who is now with the Lord, to see if he had some insight regarding this great chapter. He did.

Strangely enough, if I remember correctly, I had read his account of the meaning of the sixth chapter of Romans, which actually is the meaning of the sin nature, but what he said had not stricken a chord with me. This particular morning everything was different. It was like the Holy Spirit placed the meaning of the sin nature on a television screen, making it so simple and easy to understand.

That morning I learned the reason for so much failure in the hearts and lives of believers, and that is a tremendous truth.

When a person has done everything that he knows to do *not to fail* and fails anyway, and he doesn't know why he failed or how he failed—such presents itself as a most debilitating experience.

As I saw the truth of the sin nature, even as the Holy Spirit opened it up to me, I saw the reasons why. I remember walking back and forth across the floor in my office weeping as the Spirit of God touched my heart that particular morning.

THE APOSTLE PAUL

I later learned that the meaning of the sin nature was also the first thing given to the apostle Paul, as it regards this great redemptive work.

Romans, Chapter 5, gives us the great justification process. Then, after one is saved, the sixth chapter of Romans gives us the working of the sin nature. Sadly enough, very few Christians— even very few preachers— understand the sin nature (actually, most of the time, not at all). In that particular morning hour, the Lord opened it up to me and helped me to see some things that I had not previously known.

A few days later in our morning prayer meeting, the Lord was to give me a truth that once again was known by the apostle Paul and of course others in the early church but not so very much since then.

The Lord showed me in that morning prayer meeting that the Cross and the Cross alone was the answer to the sin nature, and all other problems as well. In fact He showed me, which I hope to give you in this volume, that every single thing we receive from the Lord comes by the means of the Cross. It's the Cross which makes everything possible. His word to me was simple, straight, and to the point:

- "The answer for which you seek is found in the Cross."
- "The solution for which you seek is found in the Cross."
- "The answer for which you seek is found *only* in the Cross."

I knew beyond a shadow of a doubt it was the Lord, and I knew that He had given me a great truth. Yet my first thought was, "How does the Holy Spirit play into all of this?" I knew He did, and in a great way, but at that stage I did not know *how*.

I had seen the world touched with the greatest harvest of souls ever, and all by the power of the Holy Spirit. I had seen tens of thousands baptized with the Holy Spirit, with the evidence of speaking with other tongues, but yet when the Lord gave me the answer respecting the Cross, the Holy Spirit wasn't mentioned. In my spirit I knew that He played a tremendous part in all of this, but all I could do was to lay it before the Lord and ask Him to complete the word. Incidentally, as the Lord took me to the great sixth chapter of Romans to explain the sin nature, He took me once again to the sixth chapter of Romans to explain the Cross.

Unfortunately, this great chapter, which I believe is the pivotal point of the entirety of the Word of God, is ignored by most Christians because they think that Paul is speaking of water baptism. Inasmuch as they have already been baptized in water, they sort of skip over this chapter as being inconsequential.

The truth is, Paul is not speaking of water baptism at all. He is speaking of us being baptized into Christ, which takes place at conversion, in other words when we are born again.

We must understand that the word *baptize* can be used figuratively or literally. Let me explain it further: John the Baptist said, *"I indeed baptize you with water unto repentance* (here, the word *baptize* is used literally)*: But he who comes after me is mightier than I, whose shoes I am not worthy to bear: He shall baptize you with the Holy Spirit and with fire"* (now he uses the word figuratively) (Mat. 3:11).

Most Christians don't know this, so they brush through this chapter, if they read it at all, and never realize the phenomenal truth that's given to us as it regards us being baptized into Christ.

KEEPING THE PROMISE

Inasmuch as this great word of the Cross had just been given to me, we were attempting to teach it over our two radio stations. We had a station in Baton Rouge, and a station in Bowling Green, Ohio.

Loren Larson was on the program with me that particular morning. As stated, we were teaching what little we then knew on the Cross of Christ.

It was only about three or four minutes before the program ended for the day, when all of a sudden something happened that was so astounding that it defies description.

I uttered a statement which came out of my mouth—a statement that I had never read in my life, never heard preached in my life, and did not know anything about—yet I knew it was from the Lord.

Through me He said: "The Holy Spirit works entirely within the parameters of the finished work of Christ, meaning the Cross, and He will not work outside of those parameters."

That was it—to the point, so very simple—but at the same time so very complex.

What did the statement mean? What was the Lord telling me? I did not really know that of which I had just stated. In fact, I did not understand what I had just stated. What did it mean?

I sat there saying nothing for a moment or two when Loren spoke up and said, "Can you give me Scripture for that?"

How could I give him Scripture when I had never heard the statement in my life? Then I looked down at my Bible, and it was opened to Romans 8. The second verse seemed to be capitalized, and seemed to come up off the page in front of my face. It stated: *"For the law of the Spirit of life in Christ Jesus has made me free from the law of sin and death"* (Rom. 8:2).

That was the Word of God for what I had just stated.

The law of which the Holy Spirit through Paul was talking about, was a law devised by the Godhead sometime in eternity past. To be sure, it is a law that will function exactly as it was designed to function.

The short phrase, *"of the Spirit of life,"* of course concerns the Holy Spirit. Sin brings death; the Holy Spirit brings life. As someone has well said, the moving of the Holy Spirit is the beginning of life. Oh yes, it is.

Then comes the great phrase *"in Christ Jesus,"* which refers to what He did for us at the Cross. I haven't taken the time to count them, but I read the other day that Paul used this phrase, or one of its derivatives, such as "in Him," "in Christ," etc., some 170 times in his 14 Epistles. As stated, it refers to what Jesus did for us at the Cross. That's the way the Holy Spirit works. He works through the Cross, by the Cross, and of the Cross. He will not work outside of the parameters of the Cross, and we of course are speaking of what Jesus there did. What Jesus did at the Cross gives the Holy Spirit the legal means to do all that He does. Actually, *"the law of the Spirit of life in Christ Jesus,"* is the only law in the universe that is stronger than *"the law of sin and death."*

DO YOU REMEMBER WHAT I PROMISED YOU?

About that time the program ended. I remember pushing up from the chair and turning to my right to leave out of the small studio when the Spirit of God came upon me again. I stopped.

The Lord said to me, "Do you remember that morning that I told you back in 1988 that I would show you things about the Holy Spirit that you did not then know?"

Of course I remembered it. There had been few days in those intervening nine years when that promise had not come to my mind.

The Lord then said, "I have just kept My promise to you, in showing you something about the Holy Spirit that you had not previously known."

I was to learn that this was really just the door that opened to much more and greater things that the Holy Spirit does for us, which I hope to give you in this volume.

Just so there will be no confusion, please allow me to repeat myself: It is the Cross of Christ that gives the Holy Spirit the legal means—the latitude—to do all that He does for us. This means that He works exclusively by and through the Cross of Christ—what Jesus there did. It also means that He will not work outside of those boundaries. So to have all of the things that the Holy Spirit can do—and there is really no limit to what He can do—the Cross of Christ must be, without fail, the object of our faith. Everything that I will say in this volume can probably be wrapped up in the simple formula that I will now give you:

- Jesus Christ is the source of all blessings that we receive from God (Jn. 1:1-3, 12, 14; 14:6).
- The Cross of Christ is the means, and the only means, by which all of these great things are done (I Cor. 1:17-18, 23; 2:2).
- With the Lord Jesus as the source, and the Cross as the means, then Christ and the Cross must ever be the object of our faith (Col. 2:10-15; Gal. 6:14).
- With our Lord as the source, the Cross as the means, and the Cross as the object of our faith, then the Holy Spirit, who works exclusively through the Cross of Christ, will work mightily on our behalf (Rom. 8:1-11; Eph. 2:13-18).

Holy Spirit, breathe on me,
Until my heart is clean;
Let sunshine fill its inmost part,
With not a cloud between.

Holy Spirit, breathe on me,
My stubborn will subdue;
Teach me in words of living flame,
What Christ would have me do.

Holy Spirit, breathe on me,
Fill me with power divine;
Kindle a flame of love and zeal,
Within this heart of mine.

Holy Spirit, breathe on me,
Till I am all Thine own,
Until my will is lost in Thine,
To live for Thee alone.

How The Holy Spirit Works

NO CONDEMNATION

NO CONDEMNATION

"THERE IS THEREFORE NOW no condemnation to them which are in Christ Jesus, who walk not after the flesh, but after the Spirit" (Rom. 8:1).

I want to use a hypothetical example to start this off and help us understand hopefully what the apostle Paul is saying.

I will use a preacher as an example, although it could pertain to anyone. The preacher of our analogy is saved, Spirit-filled, with several gifts of the Spirit flowing through him and is genuinely being used of God. However, despite all of that, he simply cannot live a victorious life in Christ. What is wrong?

In our second example, we will choose a layperson who has only been saved a few months, if that. He has heard us teach on the Message of the Cross and how the Holy Spirit works. Even though this particular person is not baptized with the Holy Spirit and has just given his heart and life to Christ a short time before, he is still able to live a victorious life—victory over the world, the flesh, and the Devil—grow in grace and the knowledge of the Lord, and be what he ought to be in Christ. What's wrong with this picture?

The preacher of our story doesn't understand anything about the Cross of Christ relative to sanctification, in other words, how we live for God. Consequently, while God can definitely use him, this particular person simply cannot live a victorious life.

The baptism with the Holy Spirit is a gift. The gifts of the Spirit fall into the same category. Consequently, the Lord will use them. Let us be quick to make this particular statement: Living a life of spiritual failure, irrespective that the Lord is using the person, will sooner or later have adverse circumstances, and very adverse circumstances. While God is patient, loving, kind, and long-suffering, still, sin always takes a deadly toll.

Now don't misunderstand, the layperson who is living a victorious life but is not yet baptized with the Holy Spirit with the evidence of speaking with other tongues, which we believe the Bible teaches and accompanies all Spirit-filled people, such a person, although living a holy life, will really not do very much for the Lord Jesus Christ.

THE IDEAL

As should be obvious, the ideal is that a person, irrespective as to whom he might be, will be baptized with the Holy Spirit with the evidence of speaking with other tongues, which is given for power (Acts 1:8), and as well understand the Cross of Christ as it regards our everyday living for God, and that the Holy Spirit works exclusively within the parameters of the finished work of Christ. That's the way it ought to be.

The sad truth is, inasmuch as most preachers around the world, even those who are being mightily used of God, don't understand the Cross of Christ relative to sanctification—how we live for God on a daily basis—and despite being used of the Lord, they simply cannot live a holy life. In other words, the sin nature will dominate such a person in some way.

THE HOLY SPIRIT

Now some may think that if the person is living a holy life, despite the fact that he isn't Spirit-filled (even though he does have the Holy Spirit as a result of regeneration when he was born-again), still, such a person—although living victorious as stated—will do very little for the cause of Christ.

The baptism with the Holy Spirit is always accompanied by the speaking with other tongues and is given to us for *service.* Power accompanies that, as we have already stated (Acts 1:8). The Holy Spirit, who comes into the heart and life of every person who is born again is meant to serve in the capacity of victory—victory over the world, the flesh, and the Devil. The first one is stated as a gift and somewhat functions automatically, at least as faith is used. The second is for victory in one's life. The ideal is that both operate.

Sadly, both groups function in the arena of spiritual defeat, simply because they do not understand God's prescribed order of victory, in other words, how the Holy Spirit works.

The first does little for the Lord, while the second one cannot live victoriously.

VICTORIOUS LIVING

Romans 8:1 opens this great chapter, which some have called the "dynamics of the Holy Spirit."

Some have stated, and I concur as well, that this verse was not translated correctly.

The translators made it seem like Paul was basing his assertion upon the saint's conduct. The truth is, Paul bases his teaching, as given to him by the Holy Spirit, upon one's position in Christ and not one's conduct. While conduct is most definitely important, it is *position* which is the key to everything taught by the great apostle.

As the subject of Romans 3 is God declaring the sinner righteous, so the theme of this eighth chapter of Romans is God making the believer holy. In other words, He seeks to bring our "standing" up to our "state." The former chapter deals with Christ's work for the sinner—justification. This eighth chapter deals with Christ's work in the believer—sanctification.

Romans 8 opens with *"no condemnation,"* and closes with *"no separation."*

The subject of Romans 5:12-21 is condemnation for all who are in Adam. The theme of this eighth chapter of Romans is no condemnation for all who are in Christ. In other words, you may have problems in your life, but if you are "in Christ" meaning that you are truly born-again, there is no condemnation despite the problems. At the same time, it is the business of the Holy Spirit to get these problems out of our lives whatever they might be.

The special Greek word used for condemnation occurs only in Romans 5:16, 5:18, and 8:1. It therefore links these two passages.

The divided state of the believer, which regrettably is the case with most believers, is glaringly obvious in Romans 7. It speaks of a terrible struggle due to the believer not knowing or understanding what Christ has actually done for him at Calvary and his standing in that finished work. However, this divided state ends in the glorious triumph of the Spirit over the flesh— that is, if the believer tenaciously clings to Christ and the Cross.

In the Greek, the word *condemnation* is *katakrima*, and means "an adverse sentence; the verdict."

WHAT ADVERSE SENTENCE OR VERDICT IS PAUL TALKING ABOUT?

He is dealing with the struggle between the flesh and the Holy Spirit in the life of the believer. Most believers may wonder at this contest between the flesh and the Holy Spirit, knowing that the Holy Spirit is God and is therefore almighty meaning that He can do anything. However, we must understand that the Holy Spirit purposely works within a different set of rules so as not to usurp authority over the free moral agency of human beings. Of course the Holy Spirit can do anything, but He will not override the direction or the thinking of the believer, even though that thinking is wrong. He will warn the believer and speak to the believer, but He will never force the believer. The Holy Spirit works within a set of guidelines that He Himself has laid down.

HE HAS DONE THIS FOR OUR BENEFIT

Let it be understood that even if the believer fully understands the Cross of Christ—referring to our sanctification and how the Holy Spirit works—this doesn't mean that Satan is going to roll over and play dead. The Evil One is going to do all that he can to steal, kill, and destroy. As long as we are alive, he will not let up. The fact is, even though one may oftentimes fail, if that believer clings to Christ, the Cross, and the Holy Spirit, then victory will ultimately be the end result. As well, we must understand that the only answer for this life is the Cross of Christ. It is not one answer among many, it is the *only* answer. The sin business is extremely serious. There is a power to sin that is so great the believer cannot throw it off within himself. He must do it God's way, and it can only be done God's way.

The Holy Spirit, as should be overly obvious, wants us to be what we ought to be, and He cannot—in fact will not—force the issue. So, unless the admonition of Romans 8 is followed regarding the way the Holy Spirit works, the flesh will triumph, which always brings condemnation. In other words, the believer fails despite the fact that he does not want to do so and is trying with all of his strength not to do so. That is the flavor of the struggle in the seventh chapter of Romans, which tells us in no uncertain terms that the believer's efforts to overcome sin within his own strength are pointless and futile. Even though a new creation in Christ Jesus, he is simply no match, at least within himself, against this monster of sin.

Let me say it again: It's not easy, and we should not insinuate that it is. As well, Satan is not going to let up, and also we may find ourselves, despite our knowledge of the Cross, failing again and again. We are not to give up because ultimately victory will be ours.

TRUTH

The believer who knows the truth and acts upon that truth allows the Holy Spirit to perform His office work, which He can only do relative to truth. The believer is now guaranteed victory, irrespective of how bad the sin or bondage may be. As the believer within himself is no match for sin, likewise sin, Satan, and death are no match for the Holy Spirit. So there is no condemnation because in following the Holy Spirit there is no failure simply because the Holy Spirit cannot fail. If we fail, and sad to say we will, that means that we have gone astray somewhere along the line. Our faith has slipped from Christ and the Cross to ourselves or something else. It's always a matter of faith, but it has to be faith in the correct object, and that correct object is Christ and the Cross.

WHY DID PAUL USE THE WORD NOW?

The word *now* tells us that this condemnation-free state is available this moment. Let's look at it: Due to repeated failure, many have come to believe that total victory is not possible in this life with such awaiting the coming resurrection when we shall be changed. However, the Holy Spirit through the apostle is loudly debunking that erroneous thought by declaring that victory is possible *now*.

To follow the prescribed methods of the Holy Spirit is ultimately to guarantee victory. To ignore these methods is to invite disaster. The word *now* emphasizes the struggle-free Christian experience offered by Christ when He said, *"Come unto Me, all you who labor and are heavy laden, and I will give you rest"* (Mat. 11:28).

When we speak of victory, we aren't speaking of sinless perfection because the Bible does not teach such. However, we are speaking of the fact that sin is not to have dominion over the believer. That's where the Holy Spirit is endeavoring to take us—no dominion, no condemnation.

IN CHRIST JESUS THE SIN DEBT IS PAID

If one is to notice, Paul uses the word *in* relative to the believer and his relationship to Christ Jesus. He didn't say "with" but rather "in" and for purpose and reason.

He is referring to the fact that one must understand and believe that when Jesus died on Calvary, upon faith the sinner is literally *"baptized into Jesus Christ,"* actually *"baptized into His death"* (Rom. 6:3).

We must quickly understand that Paul is not speaking here of water baptism, but is rather using the word *baptized* in a figurative sense because it explains the situation. It is talking about the death of Christ, and how that we died with Him.

As well, it is not a physical thing, as should be obvious, but rather that which is spiritual. Jesus did this for the sinner, and the believing sinner was actually in Christ as Christ died on Calvary.

In that death, which refers to the poured-out, perfect life of Jesus, represented in His precious shed blood, the terrible sin debt of humanity was satisfied (paid). This means that the believing sinner no longer has a debt of sin against him; consequently, Satan has no more hold or claim. Therefore, the terrible wages of sin—spiritual death; separation from God— are no longer applicable to the believing sinner. He is now united with God, which means the enmity has been removed. This is called the born-again experience (Jn. 3:3). However, as great and wonderful as that is, it is only the first part.

DOMINION OF SIN BROKEN

The second part relates to Jesus breaking the dominion of sin, which also occurred in this great sacrifice. This is primarily what is meant by Paul referring to the believer being "in Christ."

Regarding salvation, Jesus died "for the sinner." Regarding dominion over sin, the believer died "in Christ." The believer must know and understand that. Regrettably, most don't. Also, we must understand from this just how bad that sin really is. For something to take the death of the Son of God on the Cross of Calvary to satisfy its obligation lets us know that this is one more powerful force. So powerful, in fact, that we must go God's way, which is the way of the Cross, in order to have victory over this thing.

As Jesus dying for the sinner guaranteed salvation, the sinner dying in Jesus guarantees sin's dominion as broken, thereby victory over sin. So, as we have repeatedly stated, the work of Christ at Calvary was, in effect, a "double work," or one might say, a "double cure."

The first part of Jesus dying for the sinner on Calvary is known by all true believers. However, the second finished work, one might say, which actually took place at the same time as the first finished work, is not so readily known or understood by most believers. Consequently, the terrible struggle of Romans 7 continues.

WHO WALK NOT AFTER THE FLESH, BUT AFTER THE SPIRIT

First of all, what is the flesh?

The flesh pertains to that which is indicative of a human being. In other words, it is one's personal talent, education, motivation, ability, self-will, etc. In other words, what a human being can do.

The idea is that one cannot live for God by such means. Why?

When we get to Romans 8:10, we will address this more fully, but for now, I think a few words will suffice.

At the fall, everything about man was weakened, and weakened drastically. This means that what we need to do—physically and even spiritually—we cannot do it, at least within ourselves. We have to have the help of the Holy Spirit, and this is where the problem gets bigger. Most Christians little understand or don't understand at all how the Holy Spirit works and thereby try to live this life by means of the flesh.

To be sure, the flesh can be very religious, and usually is, but it is always wrong. God's way is that we place our faith entirely in Christ and the Cross, which then gives the Holy Spirit latitude to work within our lives. However, we must maintain our faith in Christ and the Cross even on a daily basis (Lk. 9:23).

The word *walk* in the Greek is *peripateo,* and it means "to live, to deport one's self, to follow." As stated, it speaks of our everyday walk, life, and living before God; in other words, how we order our behavior, which pertains to the totality of our Christian experience. If we walk after the flesh, which means we are not walking after Christ and the Cross, then we will fail every single time. Tragically, this is where most believers presently are—the flesh.

WHAT DOES IT MEAN TO
WALK AFTER THE SPIRIT?

First of all, let's see what it isn't.

Most Christians think that walking after the Spirit consists of doing spiritual things, such as prayer, church attendance, witnessing, having the gifts of the Spirit function through us, etc.

While those things are definitely important, that's not what Paul is talking about. To be frank, if we think that is walking after the Spirit—those things we've just named—then we are actually walking after the flesh.

Walking after the Spirit is when one places his faith exclusively in Christ and what Christ has done for us at the Cross, and maintains it exclusively in Christ and the Cross.

The Holy Spirit works entirely and completely by and through the Cross of Christ. It is the Cross and what Jesus there did, which gives the Holy Spirit the latitude to work. In other words, everything is by and through the Cross. That's the reason the believer must make Christ and the Cross the object of his faith, and do so continuously. That is "walking after the Spirit," which means that we can now order our behavior correctly. As we've already stated, when Paul uses the word *walk,* he is referring to how we live this life—how we order our behavior.

THE LAW OF THE SPIRIT OF LIFE IN CHRIST JESUS

"For the law of the Spirit of life in Christ Jesus has made me free from the law of sin and death" (Rom. 8:2).

I think we can say without fear of exaggeration that Romans 8:2 is the pivotal point of the entirety of the Bible. In other words, everything in the Word of God strains toward *"the law of the Spirit of life in Christ Jesus."* That's what it's all about.

Actually, the *"law of the Spirit of life in Christ Jesus"* is the most powerful law in the universe. In fact, it is the only law more powerful than the law of sin and death.

To be sure, these laws were devised by the Godhead in eternity past, and they will function exactly as designed.

"The law of the Spirit of life in Christ Jesus" is that which should govern the Christian and, in fact, will govern the Christian but only with the cooperation of the Christian.

If one is to notice, Paul has brought into this mix certain particular laws in a stronger way than ever, beginning with Romans 7:21 and continuing through Romans 8:4. Even though the greatest concentration is here, some eight laws are referred to in the book of Romans. They are as follows:

- Law of Moses (Rom. 2:12; 3:19; 7:12).
- Law of nature (Rom. 2:14-15).
- Law of faith (Rom. 3:27; 4:3-5; 11:24).
- Law of the mind (Rom. 7:16, 21, 23).
- Law of sin and death (Rom. 7:23, 25; 8:2).
- Law of righteousness (Rom. 9:31).
- Law of God (Rom. 7:22, 25).
- Law of the Spirit of life in Christ Jesus: This is the most powerful law in the universe, which alone can give victory over the law of sin and death (Rom. 8:2).

AS PAUL USES THE WORD LAW, WHAT DOES IT MEAN?

Most of the time when Paul refers to law, he is speaking of the law of Moses (Rom. 2:12-15, 17, 20, 23, 27; 3:19-21; 4:13, 16; 5:20; 7:5-8, etc.). However, he does mention other laws which we have enumerated.

The Holy Spirit through the apostle uses the word *law* in a specific sense, meaning that it is an operating and a governing principle. In this sense, Paul speaks of the *"law of faith"* (Rom. 3:27) which is contrasted with the law of works. The contrast is between the principle of faith and that of works. It is the same idea that offers the best interpretation of the word *law* in Romans 7:21, 23, 25; 8:2.

LAW AS AN OPERATING AND GOVERNING PRINCIPLE

Every law mentioned in the Bible falls into this category, even the great law of Moses. It means that the specific law is designed by God to operate in a particular manner, which will bring forth particular results. In other words, those results are unvarying. That's the reason it is called "law."

However, one cannot make these laws work against God, in other words, against His nature or against His will. These laws are made and instituted by God. They are designed to operate in a particular framework.

In other words, there is a *"law of faith"* (Rom. 3:27). This means that if a believer has faith in God, which of course must be anchored in the Word of God, certain results will be produced without fail by this law of faith. One can count on it because it is a law, and it will always function as designed.

However, that does not mean that one can take this law of faith and use it against God, i.e., against His will. These laws have not been designed to do that and cannot be used in that fashion, even though many have attempted to do so. In other words, the law of faith must give way at some point to the will of God, which is the law of God (Rom. 7:25). As well, the law of sin and death has to give way to the *"law of the Spirit of life in Christ Jesus,"* simply because this law was designed by God to be the most powerful law in the universe.

It is the same way in science. For instance, the law of gravity has to give way to the law of greater power. This speaks of any power that is strong enough to overcome the law of gravity, such as powerful engines on an airplane.

TO BE UNDER LAW

When the term "to be under law" is used in the Bible, it is speaking of the law of Moses and not the other laws mentioned. In other words, being under this law regarding New Testament believers excludes a person from the enjoyment of grace that the gospel imparts. To be under law is the opposite of being under grace and means that the person is the bondslave of the condemnation and power of sin, which Paul has already discussed in Romans 7.

However, this has nothing to do with the various other laws mentioned by Paul. To be frank, the believer strongly desires to be under *"the law of the Spirit of life in Christ Jesus"* and in fact must be under this law. As well, the believer would also strongly desire to be under the law of faith, and the law of righteousness. In fact, all of these laws mentioned by Paul constantly impact the believer in one way or another.

THE LAW OF SIN

The law of the Spirit of life in Christ Jesus, which makes real to the believer the great victory of Jesus Christ, cannot function in the life of the believer as intended if the believer is frustrating that law by obeying the law of sin at the same time. It's like pouring water into a tank made for gasoline and expecting the engine to continue to run. It won't!

What makes it so confusing is that the believer's efforts to overcome sin by his own strength and abilities—the flesh—is actually bringing upon himself the law of sin. While the efforts may be of the right motivation and not necessarily sins within themselves, they still will not work because those efforts are of the flesh and give latitude to the law of sin. Then the law of sin becomes predominant in the believer's life. This means that the sin nature is now operating at full capacity, which causes all types of problems for the believer. Yet, sad to say, this is where most modern believers actually are.

To explain what we mean when we state that the effort may not necessarily be sin within itself, I'll use fasting as an example. Fasting is scriptural. However, if we try to use fasting or even prayer to overcome sin, it won't work. Sin can be handled only at the Cross. In other words, one must evidence faith in Christ and what He did at the Cross, which then gives the Holy Spirit latitude to work within his heart and life and giving him victory over the world, the flesh, and the Devil.

As well, the law of the Spirit of life in Christ Jesus is so designed by God that it will not function or work when the believer attempts to do for himself what only the Spirit of God can do. In other words, the Holy Spirit will not override the believer's will and force him to let the Spirit take control instead of his own efforts.

FREE FROM THE LAW OF SIN AND DEATH

The question is, how does the law of the Spirit of life in Christ Jesus keep one free from the law of sin and death?

Even though we have given the following several pages back, still, it is so important that I would ask that the reader please allow us the liberty of portraying it again:

- Jesus Christ is the source of all things that we receive from God (Jn. 1:1-3, 14, 29; 14:6, 20).
- Jesus Christ is the source, but the Cross of Christ is the means, and the only means, by which all of these wonderful things come to us (Rom. 6:1-5; I Cor. 1:17-18, 23; 2:2).
- With our Lord as the source and the Cross as the means, the object of our faith must at all times be in Christ and the Cross (Col. 2:10-15).
- With Christ as our source and the Cross as our means, and the Cross of Christ the object of our faith, then the Holy Spirit, who works entirely within the parameters of the finished work of Christ, will work mightily on our behalf (Rom. 8:1-11).

This is God's way and His only way. We need to consider that carefully.

Every single person in the world is born under the dominion of the law of sin and death. It is called "original sin." This
is the law that Paul said works in the members of the physical
body of the person (Rom. 7:23). It places one in bondage and
makes the person a slave to the sin nature. Regrettably, this is
the condition of most modern Christians. How do I know that?

I know it simply because the modern church has no idea
how the Cross of Christ plays in our sanctification. And not
knowing this—not having this information—means that they
are under the control of the sin nature.

OUR POSITION IN CHRIST

Even though the law of sin and death is powerful and has
swept billions into its maw, still the law of the Spirit of life in
Christ Jesus is more powerful, in fact all-powerful. It is so powerful that there has never been a single person in history who
has come to Christ, irrespective of how sordid or bad his past
was, but that Jesus Christ took him, changed him, and made
him free from this terrible law.

The laws of God, at least as Paul mentions them here, are
not so much written laws, but rather a regulative principle that
exercises a control over the life of the believer. However, this
control must be given to the Lord by the believer. It will not
be forcibly taken.

Upon being freely given, this regulative control is exercised
by the Holy Spirit in the form of energy to the believer, both to
desire and to do God's will. This spiritual energy comes from the

life that God is, and is all made possible totally and completely by the Cross of Christ.

It is given to the believer by reason of his position in Christ Jesus but cannot be properly realized until he knows and understands his position in Christ (Rom. 6:1-5).

THE LAW OF SIN AND DEATH

An Egyptian punishment at a particular time in their history was to fasten a criminal to a corpse. The attachment continued until the death of the criminal. It was a terrible bond, as would be obvious, and more so because the man bound knew that the bond would result in his own death. This was possibly before the apostle's mind when he wrote Romans 7:24. Such a helpless and hopeless prisoner held in a bond so loathsome and fatal would cry out with anguish, "Who can deliver me from this dead body?"

This is the moral condition of all who are in Adam.

THE GLAD TIDINGS OF THE GOSPEL

Christ took this very position at Calvary, even though He had never sinned, but in effect He was paying the sin debt for all of humanity. To do this He had to die, but being God He rose from among the dead and ascended above the highest heavens, having by His death destroyed death (Heb. 2:14), abolished sin (Heb. 9:26), and exhausted the curse of the law (Gal. 3:13).

The glad tidings of the gospel are in the declaration that all, who by faith are in Christ, died and rose with Him, and consequently, there is no person and no thing that can condemn them (Rom. 6:3-5). For Christ, there is now no condemnation. He suffered its full intensity at Calvary, but He suffered that condemnation there on behalf of—and for the benefit of— all who believe upon Him. Hence, there is no condemnation for them.

A NEW POSITION

They (we) are in a new position entirely, beyond and above the reach of everything to which condemnation attaches. Where Christ and His members now stand, there can be no question of sin, wrath, condemnation, or of imputation. All such questions were settled before He ascended thither, and He is on the throne of God with His person and work accepted, because those questions were settled.

The glorious truth that liberates the believer's heart is that he is there in that glory with Christ where nothing that condemns can reach him (Eph. 2:6).

The new position in the last Adam as contrasted with the old position in the first Adam reveals that it is also a new life—a life of power, holiness, and victory. The Christian faith is not a scheme of salvation intellectually accepted, but a life of power and holiness experientially enjoyed.

Williams said, "Immanuel's destruction of sin at Calvary may become to faith a moral reality now, as it will become in the new heavens and in the new earth a physical fact; for in them righteousness alone will dwell."

FOR WHAT THE LAW COULD NOT DO

"For what the Law could not do, in that it was weak through the flesh, God sending His own Son in the likeness of sinful flesh, and for sin, condemned sin in the flesh" (Rom. 8:3).

This speaks of the law of Moses. In other words, the law of Moses could not condemn sin (destroy sin) but could only condemn the sinner, and this it did grandly.

The law said what was to be done but gave no power to do it.

The Cross of Christ is God's solution for man's dilemma, which can then function through grace.

The phrase, *"what the law could not do,"* could be rendered literally from the Greek, "the impossibility of the law." This was an impossible thing on the part of the law—that it could condemn sin by giving power to sinners in order to overcome this monster. This it could not do! In other words, the law of Moses demanded obedience, even as does all law, yet furnished man no power to obey its injunctions.

Yet this is exactly what Israel tried to force the law to do. Except for a small remnant, the entirety of generation after generation was lost in this capacity, until finally it grew so bad that they murdered their Messiah, with the resultant loss of the entirety of nationhood. As a result, they wandered as vagabonds for about 1,900 years, until finally becoming a nation again in 1948.

Regrettably, as Israel tried to force the law of Moses into a posture for which it was never intended, many of their modern disciples attempt to force faith into the same mold. God's Word must never be used against Himself. In other words, there should be no attempt to force it into that for which it was never intended.

In fact, this is the reason for all unscriptural doctrines, such as unconditional eternal security, ultimate reconciliation of all things, the modern greed gospel, works righteousness, the hundredfold return, the Jesus died spiritually doctrine, kingdom now philosophy, the 40 days of purpose effort, etc.

IN THAT IT WAS WEAK THROUGH THE FLESH

The heading means that the only power the person had in order to keep the law as given by God was his own willpower, which was woefully insufficient. As previously explained, the flesh is that which is indicative to human beings. In other words, it's one's motivation, education, personal talent, willpower, self-will—it's what a human being can do. Of themselves, these things really aren't sinful, but the sin comes in when we ignore God's way, which is Jesus Christ and Him crucified. That is what gives the Holy Spirit latitude to work, but we replace that with our own efforts, which God can never countenance.

Due to the fall, man is so weak, at least within his own power, that he can't even keep the simple laws of God laid down by the Creator, much less save himself. In fact, one of the great reasons that the law was given by God was to show man how inadequate that he is, and that he must rely upon the Savior for redemption.

In the Greek, the word *weak* is *astheneo,* and it means, "impotent; without strength."

The law of Moses was like a mirror that showed man what he is but gave man no power to change what he is. Consequently, there was no victory over sin in the law (Rom. 7:7-12).

Unfortunately, by not understanding the Cross of Christ as it regards sanctification, the far greater majority of the modern church, as previously stated, is functioning under law. It may not be the law of Moses—most of the time it isn't—but laws devised out of our own minds by our church, etc. Irrespective as to what law, the result is the same—spiritual wreckage. God's way is not the law but rather the Cross, which then gives the Holy Spirit latitude to work.

GOD SENDING HIS OWN SON

The heading refers to God's solution to man's helpless condition: his inability to save himself and his inability to keep even a simple law. Therefore, he's in dire need of a Saviour.

God sending His only Son tells us two things:

1. The tremendous love of God for lost humanity.
2. The terrible power of the bondage of sin, which could not be broken any other way than by and through Jesus Christ. God had to deliver man, that is, if man was to be delivered. He did this through the Cross and through the Cross alone (Rom. 6:3-5).

IN THE LIKENESS OF SINFUL FLESH

It says literally "of the flesh of sin." The choice of words is especially noteworthy.

Paul does not say simply, "He (Jesus) came in flesh" (I Tim. 3:16; I Jn. 4:2), for this would have expressed a bond between Christ's manhood and sin.

Not "in the flesh of sin," which would have represented Him as partaking of sin, which He did not.

Not "in the likeness of flesh," since He was really and intensely human, but "in the likeness of the flesh of sin."

This means that He was really human—conformed in appearance to the flesh whose characteristic is sin—yet sinless.

Dickson said, "Christ appeared in a body which was like that of other men insofar as it consisted of flesh, and was unlike insofar as the flesh was not 'flesh of sin.'"

AND FOR SIN

The heading means, "to atone for sin, to destroy its power, and to save and sanctify its victims." In other words, that was His purpose for coming, and to be sure, He carried out His purpose in totality.

Sin is man's problem. It is not poverty, environment, the weather, etc., but it is sin. If the church fails to understand that, it fails. Jesus went to the Cross because of the sin of mankind. He paid a price that staggers the imagination, and it was all because of the sin of humanity.

CONDEMNED SIN IN THE FLESH

The heading means that as a man—in fact the last Adam—Jesus faced all the power of sin, Satan, and death—everything that man faces and more—and never failed one time. As well, not only did He not fail, but He also destroyed the power of sin, dethroned death, and defeated Satan. In other words, He condemned sin and all its power and broke its hold over the human race (Col. 2:10-15).

Also, He did this not as deity, for such would not have sufficed, but as a man—the Man, Christ Jesus. The only help He had was the Holy Spirit, who is available to all believers.

In fact, at least as far as man was concerned, the only way that God could defeat sin and its result, which is death, was by God becoming man. Inasmuch as dominion was vested in the first Adam (Gen. 1:28; Ps. 8) and then lost through forfeiture, which in effect gave Satan dominion, it had to be purchased back by another Adam—the last Adam. All was lost in this manner, and it could only be purchased back in this manner.

THAT THE RIGHTEOUSNESS OF THE LAW MIGHT BE FULFILLED IN US

"That the righteousness of the law might be fulfilled in us, who walk not after the flesh, but after the Spirit" (Rom. 8:4).

Take the Cross out of Christianity and you have nothing left but a vapid philosophy.

The reason for the Cross was and is sin.

This tells us that the law of Moses contained righteousness, as would be obvious considering that it was given by God. However, for its righteousness to be obtained by man, perfect obedience had to be rendered, which was impossible because of the weakness of the flesh.

The phrase, *"might be fulfilled in us,"* might be translated, "find its full accomplishment in us," not merely "be performed by us." The apostle had a much deeper meaning, namely that the aim of God in giving the law might be accomplished in us—in our sanctification—which is the ultimate end of our redemption (Eph. 2:10; Col. 1:22).

THE SIGNIFICANCE OF THE LAW

I think we surely should understand from this verse just how significant the law of Moses actually was. Even though it was given exclusively to the Jews for a particular purpose and reason, it was still meant for the entirety of the world. These were God's laws and they applied to all, and I speak primarily of the moral law, i.e., the Ten Commandments. As well, this moral law could not pass out of existence because it is truth, and truth never changes.

For instance, 4,000 year ago it was wrong to steal, and it is wrong to steal presently. In fact, it will always be wrong to steal. So, God's law was righteous, and as well it had a righteousness that could be obtained by obedience, but not by man in his fallen condition. However, Jesus, as the last Adam, meaning that there will never be the need of another one, totally kept the moral law in every respect. He kept it throughout 33 and one-half years of public life, with Satan contesting Him at every turn.

As well, He took the penalty of the broken law on the Cross of Calvary. He did this as the representative man; therefore, faith in Him (Jn. 3:16) grants the believer a satisfied judgment and the position of perfect lawkeeper. In other words, at salvation we were transferred by the Lord from the position of lawbreaker to the position of lawkeeper, all because of Christ and what He did for us at the Cross and our faith in His finished work. In other words, upon faith in Him, His victory becomes our victory, which was intended.

RIGHTEOUSNESS

Upon simple faith in Christ, the vilest of human beings can become—and in fact do become—instantly righteous. Of course the world can little accept this, thinking that they can somehow earn this place and position, but their efforts are doomed to failure, for such is impossible.

Some time ago Frances and I were taking a few vacation days. During this time of rest, I was studying this very passage that we are now addressing. As I read the words, *"that the righteousness of the law might be fulfilled in us,"* the presence of God came all over me. I sat there for a few moments weeping as I sensed the Lord impressing on me the significance of this statement. It is something that only Christ can do, and something which He gloriously did do. As a result, that for which He paid such a price can now be ours by the simple act of faith.

WHO WALK NOT AFTER THE FLESH, BUT AFTER THE SPIRIT

The heading emphatically portrays to us that the righteousness of the law cannot be had by anyone who attempts to attain such by his own efforts.

The word *walk,* as we have previously stated, refers to the order of one's behavior or conduct, in other words, how we live this life.

The word *flesh* can mean the frailty of human endeavors that have been severely weakened by the fall, but in this case it refers to the indwelling evil nature. Of course, the word *Spirit* refers to the Holy Spirit.

In the Greek, the word *after* is *kata* and has as its root meaning, "down" which suggests domination.

Kenneth Wuest said, "In other words, a Christian is one who orders his behavior in such a way that it is not dominated by the evil nature (sin nature) but by the Holy Spirit."

THE BELIEVER AND THE THREE NATURES

Every believer has these three natures:
• Human nature
• Sin nature
• Divine nature

As a great portion of this chapter constantly warns the believer of the possibility and danger of walking after the flesh, such presents the great moral fact of the existence of these three natures in the believer. That is actually the theme of this chapter.

In a sense, the believer is dead, for he was crucified with Christ. Therefore, he, as a partner with Christ, enjoys all of the advantages of the partnership acquired by Christ before he was brought into it. This is not necessarily an experience; it is rather a divine operation apprehended and enjoyed by faith.

However, the believer is always very conscious that his sinful nature is not dead—between it and the new spiritual nature (divine nature) he received at conversion (Eph. 1:13), there is a deadly warfare between the two that really never stops.

If the carnal nature were actually dead as some claim, it would not be necessary to urge Christian people not to make provision to gratify its appetites (Rom. 13:14).

WHAT DOES WALKING AFTER THE FLESH MEAN?

It means we're trying to live this life for the Lord by means other than the Cross, and irrespective as to what those means might be, we will fail.

WHAT IS WALKING AFTER THE SPIRIT?

Walking after the Spirit of course refers to the Holy Spirit and the believer placing his or her faith exclusively in Christ and the Cross and maintaining it exclusively in Christ and the Cross. That is walking after the Spirit.

THE TEACHING OF THE NEW NATURE

The new nature (divine nature) is energized by the Holy Spirit, hence our walking after Him. This teaches us that the Christian may enjoy such victory because the Word of God asserts its existence. Actually, it is a moral experience so liberating that the fact of indwelling sin may become to the believer only a matter of knowledge rather than a painful fact of consciousness.

In other words, while it is true that this contest between the flesh and the Spirit is unending, if we follow after Christ exactly as we should, which refers to ever making the Cross of Christ the object of our faith, we are made to enjoy a rest that is actually beyond comprehension. Of course, let us say it again, this means ever making the Cross of Christ the object of our faith. There is no answer for sin except by the Cross. Once we function as we should while we do fight, it is only the good fight of faith.

Regrettably, most Christians have the opposite and therefore sad experience of repeated failure because they do not understand the Cross of Christ relative to our sanctification. They are painfully conscious of this principle of evil lodged in their nature, while the existence of the new nature (divine nature) within them is a matter of belief because it is declared in the Scriptures, but regrettably it is not fully enjoyed by most.

Thus Romans 8:2 forms its keynote. It asserts the existence of these two natures in the believer but declares that the new spiritual nature liberates from the old carnal nature. So the subject of this chapter is not so much the forgiveness of sins or justification from sin, but rather liberation from the power of sin in order to live a life of sanctification.

THE HOLY SPIRIT

One cannot help but notice the emphasis that Paul places on the Holy Spirit. Why?

The simple fact is, as believers we need the leading, guidance, and empowerment of the Holy Spirit 24 hours a day, seven days a week in all things that we do. The Holy Spirit is God. Consequently, He is all-powerful and all-knowing meaning that He knows everything—past, present, and future. As well, He is everywhere. The sad fact is, most believers receive precious little of what the Holy Spirit can do and abundantly so. The fault is not His, but rather ours.

Most believers have the idea that whatever needs to be done, the Holy Spirit will just automatically do it. But consider the following: What I've just stated is not correct—the Holy Spirit does not automatically do anything. It is really dependent on us. What do I mean by that?

The Holy Spirit will not override our will, and He will not force us into any direction. He will speak to us, touch us, and do all within His power to help us, without forcing us to do anything. If our believing is wrong, this hinders Him greatly.

SERVICE

While it is definitely true that the Holy Spirit comes into the heart and life of the believing sinner at the moment of salvation—that is the regeneration of the Spirit and not the baptism with the Spirit.

There is a vast difference in being "born of the Spirit," and being "baptized with the Spirit." Every believer in the world has the Holy Spirit as it regards regeneration. To have the power of the Spirit, one must be baptized with the Spirit, which is always accompanied by the speaking with other tongues (Acts Chpts. 2, 8, 9, 10, 19).

Without the baptism with the Holy Spirit, one is not going to do very much for the Lord. I didn't say that nothing can be done, but I am saying that not much can be done. At the same time, and which we have stated previously in this volume, one can be baptized with the Holy Spirit and even used of the Lord—and used greatly—but still not be able to live a victorious life within himself. Millions are in that posture, and they don't understand why.

For the Holy Spirit to work for us and with us, helping us to overcome the world, the flesh, and the Devil, the faith of the individual must ever have as its object Christ and Him crucified—that is a must (I Cor. 1:17, 18, 23; 2:2; Gal. 6:14; Col. 2:10-15).

All sin is addressed at the Cross and is addressed no place else. In other words, the believer is not going to find victory over sin until he places his or her faith exclusively in Christ and what Christ has done for us at the Cross. Then the Holy Spirit with His almighty power can go to work in our lives, giving us victory over sin, and in every capacity. No, I'm not meaning sinless perfection, for the Bible does not teach that. I am stating that dominion of sin, which is the problem, will be forever broken (Rom. 6:14).

THE FLESH

The Christian who is fighting in the flesh, even though very sincere, is not really helping the situation, but is actually severely hurting his cause. Once the believer knows the truth of what Christ has done, and has faith in that great and wondrous work, the Holy Spirit can take over and do all that needs to be done. This makes the Christian life a tremendously pleasurable experience. Otherwise it can be hell on earth, and that is not an exaggeration!

What do you think it was for Paul before he learned this great truth when he said, *"O wretched man that I am! Who shall deliver me from the body of this death?"* (Rom. 7:24)

The believer must understand that the Holy Spirit works entirely within the framework of the Cross of Christ. In other words, it's what Jesus did at the Cross that gives the Holy Spirit the legal means to do all that He does for us. He doesn't require much of us, but He does require one thing, and that is for our faith to be perpetually in Christ and the Cross—and maintained in Christ and the Cross. Then He can work. Otherwise He would be helping us commit spiritual adultery, which He will not do.

Standing on the promises of Christ my King,
Through eternal ages let His praises ring,
Glory in the highest I will shout and sing,
Standing on the promises of God.

Standing on the promises that cannot fail,
When the howling storms of doubt and fear assail,
By the living Word of God I shall prevail,
Standing on the promises of God.

Standing on the promises I now can see,
Perfect, present cleansing in the blood for me;
Standing in the liberty where Christ makes free,
Standing on the promises of God.

Standing on the promises of Christ the Lord,
Bound to Him eternally by love's strong cord,
Overcoming daily with the Spirit's sword,
Standing on the promises of God.

Standing on the promises I cannot fall,
Listening every moment to the Spirit's call,
Resting in my Saviour as my all in all,
Standing on the promises of God.

How The Holy Spirit Works

THE FLESH AND THE SPIRIT

CHAPTER THREE

THE FLESH AND THE SPIRIT

"FOR THEY WHO ARE after the flesh do mind the things of the flesh; but they who are after the Spirit the things of the Spirit" (Rom. 8:5).

FOR THEY WHO ARE AFTER THE FLESH DO MIND THE THINGS OF THE FLESH

While of course Romans 8:5 can apply to the unredeemed, Paul is speaking to the redeemed. He is portraying the struggle between the flesh and the Spirit and how the believer is in one or the other or somewhere in between.

The Greek has it this way: "For those who are habitually dominated by the flesh put their mind on the things of the flesh." The flesh, as it is used here, pertains to the ability of the human being—education, motivation, personal talent, personal ability, or self-will. In other words, it is what a human being can do.

Unfortunately, due to the fact of not understanding the Cross of Christ relative to our sanctification—how we live for

God on a daily basis—virtually the entirety of Christendom is trying to live for God by means of the flesh. Consequently, their entire thought process functions in that capacity. In other words, they function with more and more flesh.

In the Greek, the word *mind* is *phroneo,* and means "to exercise the mind, or have a sentiment or opinion." Consequently, it means that the believer who functions in the flesh has an improper understanding of the Word of God concerning this tremendous problem. Therefore, he is attempting to gain victory in all of the wrong ways. He is not necessarily doing it purposely or unintentionally; nevertheless, the end result is the same: domination by the flesh, i.e., the sin nature.

Yet many simply do not believe what Paul is saying here, which means that unbelief characterizes their thinking. This is more prominent than most realize—unbelief.

BUT THEY WHO ARE AFTER THE SPIRIT THE THINGS OF THE SPIRIT

The heading presents the very opposite of the previous phrase.

That which is after the Spirit is that which is after the Word of God. This pertains to the Cross of Christ which pertains to the way the Holy Spirit works. He cannot nor will the Holy Spirit function except according to the blueprint which is the Word of God. While He will definitely help the seeking believer find the truth, He will not force such upon the disinterested or those who function in unbelief. What are the things of the Spirit?

In the Greek, the word *things* is *logos* and means "something said, including the thought, by implication a topic (subject of discourse), also reasoning (the mental faculty) or motive, and above all the divine expression, i.e., Christ."

So, who Jesus is, what Jesus said, and what Jesus did is the eternal logos, i.e., the things of the Spirit. Even though it pertains to all things relative to Christ, more particularly it refers to the great truth of Him breaking the dominion of sin (at least in this case).

If the believer sets his mind upon this of which Jesus has done, and believes it with all of his heart (we continue to speak of the Cross), he will receive the things of the Spirit, which will fall out ultimately to total victory, in this case victory over sin.

While the word *things* has the same connotation or meaning concerning the flesh, it is there inverted. It presents the believer, who should be speaking the words of Christ, or the Spirit, instead speaking words of the flesh, which pertains to error, and most likely religious error. It is difficult to explain, but in its most simplistic form it means that the believer speaks the words of Christ versus the believer who does not. However, the manner in which Paul made the statement needs more explanation.

MENTAL AFFIRMATION

It is possible for a believer to know this truth as laid out in Romans, but actually knows it only in his or her intellect. Consequently, he gives a mental assent or affirmation to this truth but really does not know it experientially. In other words, it is not in his heart, and consequently will bring forth few results if any.

To be frank, there are many who mistake mental affirmation for faith and are confused when it does not bring forth positive results. True knowledge of the things of God pertains not only to a knowledge of the intellect but, as well, that which gets down into one's spirit. This is how true faith springs forth.

So the favorite statement of many people—"I've tried that, and it doesn't work" —is the tip-off that true faith is lacking with the individual only giving mental assent to the subject at hand. Many people attempt to learn the things of God, and above all the Word of God, even as they would learn arithmetic, but it is not to be learned or understood in that fashion. It is only by revelation, and many times revelation comes by desperation.

Jesus, the eternal logos, must become a part of one's very spirit and being. In fact, when one has true faith in God, which refers to faith in Christ and the Cross, it is quite possible for him to exhibit faith, but little explain what he is exhibiting. On the other hand, oftentimes those who have a mere mental assent can, in fact, properly explain what they believe but obtain few results.

DOMINATION

"After the Spirit" is a way of life. That's the reason Paul used the term *"dominated by the Spirit."* The word *after* should have been translated, "dominated" for that is the actual Greek word used here.

Consequently, it could be translated "for they who are dominated by the flesh do mind the things of the flesh; but they who are dominated by the Spirit, the things of the Spirit." However, there is a difference in the way the word *dominated* is used.

The domination of the flesh sooner or later goes into compulsion. In other words, the individual is compelled by this domination to do those things that are wrong, which Paul outlines in the seventh chapter of Romans. However, the word *dominated,* as it is used concerning the Holy Spirit, is the exact opposite. While the Holy Spirit will definitely dominate the believer, it is only when the believer freely gives control to the Spirit. In essence, the Spirit will never force a believer to give Him control.

As well, the Holy Spirit dominates the believer only in the sense of that which is good for the believer, which is the very opposite of the flesh. He has our good at heart, and constantly pushes forth toward the realization of such good.

How wonderful it is to be led by the Spirit, guided by the Spirit, empowered by the Spirit, taught by the Spirit, and to be *"after the Spirit."*

Let us say it again: The Holy Spirit works exclusively within the framework of the finished work of Christ. He will not work outside of those parameters, so to speak. This means that the Cross of Christ gives the Holy Spirit the legal means to do all that He does. It requires of us that our faith ever be in Christ and the Cross, and ever maintained in Christ and the Cross, and then the Holy Spirit will work mightily within our hearts and lives. Otherwise we greatly limit Him by placing our faith elsewhere.

FOR TO BE CARNALLY MINDED IS DEATH

"For to be carnally minded is death; but to be spiritually minded is life and peace" (Rom. 8:6).

To be carnally minded is to trust in that which is of the flesh, which means that it's not of Christ and Him crucified.

To be spiritually minded is to place one's faith exclusively in Christ and the Cross and maintain it exclusively in Christ and the Cross.

This springs back to the flesh in Romans 8:5. In the Greek, "carnally minded" is "to phronema tes sarkos" and means literally, "the mind of the flesh." Again, flesh refers to the evil or sin nature. While they are not the same, when a person functions in the flesh, the sin nature is going to rule such a person.

The word *death* speaks of spiritual death, i.e., separated from God. So the question must be asked, Can the believer continue indefinitely following after the flesh?

Yes, a believer can continue indefinitely following after the flesh, but such proves to be a miserable existence. If the believer doesn't understand the Cross of Christ relative to sanctification—how we live for God, how we order our behavior, how we have victory over the world, the flesh, and the Devil—then such a believer is going to function after the flesh. There are only two places—the flesh and the Spirit. Let us say it again: if the Cross is not properly understood, then the flesh is the only other alternative.

The truth is that most Christians, and I speak of those who truly love the Lord, have never really known what it is to experience Bible Christianity. They are struggling with problems in their lives and have done so almost the entirety of their Christian experience. That's not God's way, but it is the way of those who function outside of the Cross.

THE FLESH AND DEATH

What did Paul mean by the statement, *"For to be carnally minded is death?"*

To be carnally minded means that a person is not being led of the Holy Spirit. This means that his faith is in something other than Christ and the Cross, which means that such a person is going to be constantly failing the Lord. He will find that death is attached to everything he does. His plans die. His efforts are wrecked. Instead of victory, it is defeat. Satan steals, kills, and destroys, and we must never forget that. If the sin nature is ruling, death is always attached to the word *sin*. That means sooner or later, whatever it is that we touch, and I mean whatever, ultimately dies.

Let me say it again: There is only one way for the child of God, and that is the way of the Cross. If we try any other way, no matter how religious it might be, it will result in wreckage, i.e., death.

Please understand that when Paul uses the word *death*, he is speaking of destruction as it regards every single thing the carnal mind does. As previously stated, it all leads to wreckage, hurt, pain, suffering, and ultimately death. Of course, Satan wants such a believer to just give up, quit trying to live for God in any fashion (which many do) and ultimately die and go to hell—the ultimate death. But it doesn't have to be that way. God's way is the Cross, and when you begin to make the Cross of Christ the object of your faith exclusively, you will find things beginning to change for the better. It will be a struggle because Satan doesn't want you going in that direction. But if you will persist—meaning that you won't give up and you won't throw it over—then you are going to find victory.

BUT TO BE SPIRITUALLY MINDED IS LIFE AND PEACE

This presents the most glorious, wonderful, and fulfilling life that one could ever know. This is what living is really all about. This is that which only God can give, and He reserves it for those who love Him and believe in His great and glorious name. While it is for anyone, still the requirements of faith must be met.

The words "spiritually minded" in the Greek are "to phronema tou pneumatos" and means literally "the mind possessed by the Spirit." That's a mind controlled or dominated by the Holy Spirit.

Such a person possesses the life that God is—life and peace.

The word *peace* as it is used here, means "to bind together that which has been separated." Thus the believing sinner is bound together with God and His life after having been separated by sin. Please remember, the only place for sin, and I mean the only place, is the Cross.

The life and peace spoken of here cannot be purchased with money, attained by education, discovered through scientific theory, or earned by religious works. It is a free gift from God, but only when our faith is properly placed. Never forget that!

Our faith must be in Christ and what Christ has done for us at the Cross. Then the Holy Spirit will work mightily in our hearts and lives, giving us victory in every capacity, which He alone can do; however, it's all predicated upon our faith in Christ and what He has done for us at the Cross. It is the Cross of Christ meaning what He there did that makes everything possible.

This is what opened the door to the treasure house of God: the Cross, the Cross, the Cross!

TWO WILLS

There are two wills contrasted in Romans 8:5-8: the will of the carnal nature and the will of God. The carnal will, being independent of God's will, is consequently hostile to it and cannot be otherwise.

Therefore, all who are governed by the carnal will cannot please God so long as they are thus governed, be they ever so religious, moral, cultivated, or noble. It's not that God takes no pleasure in noble actions performed by unconverted men, but it's that He cannot take pleasure in and accept religious worship and meritorious actions designed to purchase His favor, which are prompted by the carnal mind. Hence, He rejected Cain's worship and offerings.

All who are controlled by the carnal will set their affections upon gratifying it. The opposite is true in the case of those controlled by the divine will. Control by the one ends in death, the other in life.

BECAUSE THE CARNAL MIND IS ENMITY AGAINST GOD

"Because the carnal mind is enmity against God: For it is not subject to the law of God, neither indeed can be" (Rom. 8:7).

The flesh cannot please God in any capacity. It is faith alone in Christ and the Cross that pleases God (Heb. 11:5-6).

Let us say it again: the carnal mind is the mind that is fastened onto that which is not Christ and the Cross.

One might say that the weapons being used by such a believer are his willpower, or even spiritual things that are good within themselves, but will not perform the intended task of freedom.

Even though the believer does not think as such, attempting to use his willpower to overcome sin constitutes a carnal mind. It would actually be the same, were he using quite legitimate principles such as confession, the laying on of hands, etc. One can name several other great biblical principles also.

We are certainly not saying that these biblical principles are wrong. In reality they are right, and even very much right. However, to use such attributes in the capacity of that which we speak—to overcome sin—even as valuable as they are, is the same as a carpenter attempting to use a handsaw instead of a hammer to drive nails. It simply will not work because the handsaw was not made for that purpose.

Satan tricks us by these things simply because they are very good, and actually bless us greatly, but sadly and regrettably we find that they do not bring us the victory that we seek, and in fact must have.

Yet the reader must ask, How could these things that are so right within themselves, even though used wrongly, be declared as enmity against God?

FOR IT IS NOT SUBJECT TO THE LAW OF GOD, NEITHER INDEED CAN BE

In the Greek, the word *enmity* is *echthra* and means "hostility." In this case, hostility against God.

The reader who is caught in this trap might quickly exclaim that he has no hostility against God, but rather the very opposite. That is correct, but at the same time, incorrect.

The answer is found in the following: It means that whatever is being done, whatever it might be, is not in God's prescribed order, and therefore presents the person not going God's way, which generates hostility, whether intended or not. Our Lord has gone to tremendous trouble, to say the least, to afford redemption for mankind. It cost Him His life, given over as a sacrifice. In other words, the price was paid at Calvary's Cross. That is the answer—Christ and the Cross.

When we try to go another way, whatever that other way might be, it should be obvious why it angers God. In the first place, it won't work. In the second place, we are actually forcing ourselves against God, in other words, against His will. His will is Christ and the Cross and none other. Anything else, no matter how right it may be in its own way, angers Him, and it should be understandable as to why.

WHAT IS THE LAW OF GOD?

Paul said that the carnal mind *"is not subject to the law of God, neither indeed can be."*

The law of God, I think, could possibly be divided into two ways:

1. In the Old Testament, at least after the law was given, it was the Ten Commandments, or one might say the law of Moses.

2. At the present time, at least since the Cross, one might say that it is "Jesus Christ and Him crucified." In fact, the entirety of the story of the Bible is the story of Jesus Christ and Him crucified. That is the Word of God. That is God's way. It is the law of God.

God's plan is the Cross of Christ. He cannot sanction another plan and cannot condone another plan. Anything that is of another way, no matter how sincere the person might be, presents itself as hostility toward God. We don't think of such in that fashion, but that's what it is, and to be sure it is very serious.

It doesn't matter what it is, if it's not Christ and Him crucified and our faith in that finished work, whatever it is, it is wrong. God can never sanction such.

SO THEN THEY WHO ARE IN THE FLESH

"So then they who are in the flesh cannot please God" (Rom. 8:8).
The flesh is that which operates outside of the Cross. Such
a direction cannot please God.

As we have explained, the flesh is that which is indicative of
a human being. It refers to our self-will, education, motivation,
personal talent, will power, etc. That is what Paul means by "the
flesh." Please understand that the flesh can be very religious and
thereby very deceitful. The idea is that everything that God
gives mankind is that which He originates. God cannot accept
anything that man originates, and I mean nothing. The idea is
that sinful man simply cannot originate anything that is godly
or holy, no matter how hard he tries. This is man's great failure:
we think we can, so we keep trying even as we keep failing.

God has a way of salvation; it is simple faith in Christ. When
we try to come another way—by fashioning something else,
belonging to a certain church, or performing certain good
works—it is hostility toward God, which God can never accept.
These works are the bane of humanity. It's all flesh and not of God.

Everything that is of God is faith, and we speak of faith in
Christ and what Christ has done for us at the Cross.

CANNOT PLEASE GOD

It is to the point and designed to be that way. Anything and
everything that's of the flesh, no matter how religious it might
be, simply cannot please God.

God does not look for ability, talent, resources, or self-will in man as a requirement, but rather the very opposite, which is a brokenness before Him.

In effect, this says man knows that within himself he deserves nothing good from God (Isa. 66:2; Lk. 18:14). Actually, biblical faith does not really function very well outside the sphere of biblical humility.

THE FLESH AND DISPLEASING GOD

As we have stated, flesh basically speaks of man's frailty, inability, and weakness—even impossibility regarding spiritual things. Inasmuch as humanity is fallen, that means that within the flesh man has nothing good, can do nothing good, and cannot come up with anything that pleases God, as should be obvious. Yet we seem to keep trying.

The whole idea is that if man tries anything within himself, whether a believer or otherwise, God simply cannot accept such. This is at least one of the reasons that God hates self-righteousness to such an extent, because it originates with the flesh and man's self-efforts or self-will. Consequently, it is coming from a poisoned source, which can never be accepted by God. As well, if self-righteousness becomes the attitude of a believer, the flesh from such a source is just as hateful to God as it is in an unbeliever—and actually far worse!

In the first place, the believer should know that anything he has that is any good has come from God and originated totally with God. This means that God does not need any help. In fact, if man, even converted man, tempts to help God in these areas, which all of us have tried to do at one time or another, it only tends to frustrate the grace of God and therefore sully that which the Holy Spirit is attempting to do within our hearts and lives.

What we're speaking of here is the sanctification process. The godliest believer in the world cannot sanctify himself. It simply cannot be done. We must go God's way, and that way always is Christ and the Cross.

As the flesh keeps much of the human family from coming to God, likewise the flesh is the greatest hindrance to the believer. The temptation is always very heavy to add something to what Jesus has already done, to take away from what He has already done, or to substitute something altogether in its place. However, no matter how consecrated such an effort may be, it does not please God, and in fact, *cannot* please God in any capacity.

THE PERSONAL EXPERIENCE OF PAUL

When Paul wrote these words, he was writing something of which he knew firsthand. For a particular time in his Christian life, he attempted to overcome sin with the efforts of the flesh, his own willpower, ability, etc. It did not work, even as it cannot work. So he knew firsthand of the terrible dangers and the futility of such an effort, and as well how it displeases God for His children to attempt such.

I look back in my own life and I tend to grieve when I realize how I have personally fallen into this trap so many times,

and how it caused me so much heartache, troubles, and difficulty. Even though I did it in ignorance, the result was the
same: great hurt.

Paul learned, as so many of us have, that every effort by the
flesh—no matter how well-intentioned, motivated, or loaded
down with Scriptures and religious effort—only tends to make
the situation worse, with sin even more pronounced. In other
words, instead of climbing out of the hole, we tend to sink deeper
(Rom. 7:15).

THERE ARE MANY REASONS FOR THIS

First of all, as we have stated, when one tends to make this
effort, one is attempting to solve the problems of the flesh with
the flesh, which is impossible. He is attempting to assuage a
poisoned situation with water from a poisoned spring, so to
speak. Irrespective of that, even if it was not poisoned and
polluted, man simply does not have the strength to overcome
sin within himself. It just cannot be done due to the fall. The
problem is of far greater magnitude than any human being
could ever begin to realize. It is so bad, in fact, that God had
to become man, literally become a human sacrifice, i.e., a sin
offering, in order for the terrible sin debt to be paid and its
dominion broken.

As well, what Jesus did at Calvary completed the task of victory and deliverance over sin in totality. Nothing can be added,
as nothing needs to be added. In fact, when we try to add something, as previously stated, we insult God.

AN EXAMPLE

To use a crude analogy, let's say that a man owed a billion dollars at the bank and, being flat broke, had absolutely no way to pay this terrible debt. Then a wealthy benefactor stepped in and paid the entirety of the debt. He also deposited a billion dollars in cash in the same bank, and told the bank administrators that the man who had formerly owed this terrible debt was now free to write checks to his heart's content on this new account.

Of course the man was now very elated that this terrible debt had been paid, and him no longer owing anything. As well, he was told of the tremendous amount of money that was in the bank, and that he was free to write checks on that account for whatever he needed.

Then the man had to purchase a piece of land that cost a million dollars. To purchase this land, he went to the bank, opened a new account, and deposited $10, which was separate from the huge account that was already available to him in the bank. He wrote a million dollar check on his new account that he had just opened when in reality he only had $10 in it.

FOOLISH DIRECTION

The banker said to him, "Why are you doing this? Your $10 in the bank will not cover a million dollar check. Besides, you don't need to do this considering that we have a billion dollars in this bank on which you can write as many checks as you like. I have also been told by your benefactor that if you exhaust this billion dollars, he will instantly replenish it with as much as is needed."

Considering what the benefactor had done for this man, I should think it would be obvious that he would not be too very much pleased at the foolish personal actions of this individual regarding finances. It is the same with the Lord. Even though our illustration is very crude, this is exactly what we believers have done many times. We have tried to take our two cents and purchase what only a billion dollars could obtain, which has already been provided, at least if we are allowed to use such an illustration.

Everything we need has already been done by Christ. So why do we insult Him by attempting to do it all over again ourselves, which is impossible anyway?

The problem in most cases is ignorance. In other words, the believer simply does not know or understand the part that the Cross plays in our sanctification, so he tries other methods, which never work. Then we have the problem of unbelief. Believe it or not, there are many Christians who simply do not believe that the Cross of Christ plays such a part in their everyday experience with the Lord, so they attempt to assert other things. Either way, the end result is going to be wreckage. If we do not do it God's way, which is the way of the Cross, it simply will not get done.

BUT YOU ARE NOT IN THE FLESH

"But you are not in the flesh, but in the Spirit, if so be that the Spirit of God dwell in you. Now if any man have not the Spirit of Christ, he is none of his" (Rom. 8:9).

God's way is the Cross of Christ. He has no other way because no other way is needed. Everything was addressed at the Cross, not only justification, but sanctification as well.

In one sense of the word, the heading is asking the question, "Since you are now a believer and no longer depending on the flesh, why are you resorting to the flesh?" Unfortunately, virtually the entirety of the church world, and I speak of those who truly love the Lord, are operating in the flesh.

How do I know that?

If the believer doesn't understand the Cross of Christ relative to our sanctification—how we live for God on a daily basis and how we have victory over sin—then such a believer is going to function in the flesh. There are only two ways that he can function: the flesh or the Holy Spirit. As we have said several times in this volume, the modern church simply does not know how to live for God. I realize that's quite a statement, but sadly and regrettably it is true. To understand how to live for the Lord, one must without fail understand the Cross of Christ relative not only to his salvation, but as well to his sanctification. To be frank, most believers have never heard of the Cross of Christ relative to sanctification. So, as already stated, they resort to the flesh.

BUT IN THE SPIRIT

The phrase, *"but in the Spirit,"* in effect is saying, "You now have the Holy Spirit to help you."

As we have previously stated, the Holy Spirit does not require much of us, but He does require one thing, and on that He will not bend. He demands that our faith be exclusively in Christ and the Cross, and then He will work mightily within our lives. The Holy Spirit is God. There is nothing that He cannot do. However, He will never violate the free moral agency of anyone. As a believer, if you desire to resort to the flesh, He will speak to you and deal with you, but He will not force the issue. Due to the fact that the way to victory, which is the Cross, has been so little preached in the last several decades, most Christians simply don't know what the Bible says about the matter (Rom. 6:3-4; I Cor. 1:17, 18, 23; 2:2; Col. 2:10-15).

Before the Cross, the Holy Spirit could not come into the hearts and lives of believers to abide permanently. He could come into the hearts of certain individuals such as prophets to help them carry out that which they were called to do, but when that was finished, He would leave.

WHY?

It was because the blood of bulls and goats could not take away sins (Heb. 10:4), and with that being the case, the sin debt remained, which of course greatly hindered the Holy Spirit. Likewise, before the Cross, when a believer died his soul and spirit could not be taken into heaven, but rather was taken down into paradise, which was very close to the burning side of hell. Actually, they were only separated by a great gulf (Lk. 16). Once again, it was because animal blood was woefully insufficient.

However, when Jesus paid the full price on Calvary's Cross, this changed everything. Now the Holy Spirit can live permanently, which He does, in the heart and life of every believer (Jn. 14:16-17).

IF SO BE THAT THE SPIRIT
OF GOD DWELL IN YOU

The heading, in essence, says "provided that," or "assuming that"—assuming that the Spirit of God dwells in the believer, which He most definitely does.

In the Greek, the word *dwell* is *oikeo* and means, "to live or dwell in a certain place as your home." The Holy Spirit is not only resident in the believer in the sense of position in him, but He is actively at home in him, living in him as His home.

A MINISTRY TO PERFORM

It further means that the Holy Spirit is not in us just to be there, but rather has a ministry to perform in the believer, namely to give the believer victory over sin and produce His own fruit. He gives the believer victory over sin by making real to him and energizing within him the great truth and fact of what Christ did at Calvary. This—together with the presence of the imparted divine nature in the believer and the fact that God has broken the power of the evil nature—puts the believer out of the sphere of the evil nature and within the sphere of the Holy Spirit. Consequently, the believer is therefore not in the grip of the evil nature, but under the control of the Holy Spirit as he yields himself to Him.

However, these things that we have said are the ideal, meaning what is supposed to be. Too often the believer does not know the full truth of what Christ has done for him at Calvary, which gives the Holy Spirit little to work on and work with. As well, most believers do not yield to the Holy Spirit very well either, thus taking control out of His hands. So, the truth is that the Holy Spirit in most believers can only do and be to a limited degree, in comparison to what really can be done. In other words, most of us live far beneath what we can truly be in Christ. We tie the hands of the Holy Spirit, grieving and wounding Him, and actually allowing Him very little latitude within our lives. That's the reason we have said that His work is potential—only what we will allow Him to do, which too often is not very much.

NOW IF ANY MAN HAVE NOT THE SPIRIT OF CHRIST, HE IS NONE OF HIS

This refers to the Holy Spirit. In other words, it is not possible for a person to be truly saved without the Holy Spirit dwelling in him. Some have thought that the *"Spirit of Christ"* referred to Christ's personal Spirit, but that is incorrect.

Paul is merely saying that the Holy Spirit coming in to dwell within the heart and life of the believer is made possible only by what Christ did at Calvary. There Jesus satisfied the terrible sin debt, which meant that Satan no longer held a claim on anyone who evidenced faith in Christ. Consequently, since the day of Pentecost, the Spirit of God does not merely come to be with believers, but rather to dwell in believers (Jn. 14:17).

So, Paul is saying to failing believers that if they claim the Holy Spirit is not within their lives helping them, then that means they are not even saved, because if they are saved, the Holy Spirit is there and is ready to do what He is there to do.

THE TWOFOLD WORK OF THE SPIRIT

The Holy Spirit is meant to function in every capacity of our lives and living, giving us leading and guidance—especially guidance into all truth—with the fruit of the Spirit being developed. However, the greatest work that He performs in this capacity is to give us victory over sin. He does this strictly by and through our faith in Christ and what Christ has done for us at the Cross.

In other words, it is the Cross of Christ that gives the Holy Spirit the legal means to do all that He does (Rom. 8:2). While the Bible does not teach sinless perfection, it most definitely does teach that sin is not to have dominion over us (Rom. 6:14). The Holy Spirit alone can carry this out. In fact, the Holy Spirit is jealous, one might say, over any territory in our lives occupied by the Evil One.

TO EARNESTLY OR PASSIONATELY DESIRE

James said:

> *Do you think that the Scripture says in vain* (James was quoting several Scriptures [Gen. 15:6; 49:10; Ex. 17:6; Ps. 78:16; Ezek. 47:9; Joel 2:28-29]), *the Spirit who dwells in us lusts*

to envy? (This refers to the Holy Spirit, which means that the word *Spirit* should have been capitalized. The word *'lusts'* here means 'to earnestly or passionately desire.' Of what is He envious, and what does He passionately desire? The Holy Spirit is envious of any control the fallen nature might have over the believer, and is passionately desirous that He control all of our thoughts, words, and deeds. He is desirous of having the believer depend upon Him for His ministry to Him, so that He might discharge His responsibility to the one who sent Him, namely God the Father (James 4:5) (The Expositor's Study Bible).

THE BAPTISM WITH THE HOLY SPIRIT

After the believing sinner is saved, meaning that the Holy Spirit has regenerated such a person, then that believer should go on and be baptized with the Holy Spirit, which will always be accompanied by the speaking with other tongues (Acts 2:4). It must be understood that there is a great difference in being "born of the Spirit" and being "baptized with the Spirit."

The baptism with the Spirit is to help the believer carry out the work of God—to help the preacher preach, the teacher teach, the singer sing, and to help us in our worship. If you are a teacher, He'll help you to be a better teacher, a better truck driver, a better accountant, a better painter, etc. As well, He gives us power against the forces of darkness that would attempt to stop our work for God. Without the baptism with the Holy Spirit, there isn't going to be much anointing of the Spirit, if any.

So, the Holy Spirit functions in two capacities: power for service and power in our lives for victory over sin. Regrettably, He is given very little latitude in the hearts and lives of most believers to do anything. This is sad but oh so true.

Glory hallelujah, I shall not be moved,
Anchored in Jehovah, I shall not be moved,
Just like a tree that's planted by the waters,
I shall not be moved.

In His love abiding, I shall not be moved,
And in Him confiding, I shall not be moved,
Just like a tree that's planted by the waters,
I shall not be moved.

Though all hell assail me, I shall not be moved,
Jesus will not fail me; I shall not be moved,
Just like a tree that's planted by the waters,
I shall not be moved.

Though the tempest rages, I shall not be moved,
On the Rock of Ages, I shall not be moved,
Just like a tree that's planted by the waters,
I shall not be moved.

How The Holy Spirit Works

THE BODY AND THE SPIRIT

THE BODY AND THE SPIRIT

"AND IF CHRIST BE in you, the body is dead because of sin; but the Spirit is life because of righteousness" (Rom. 8:10).

AND IF CHRIST BE IN YOU

The fall made it impossible for the flesh to do anything that God can accept. It is the Holy Spirit who does the doing, which is made possible by the Cross of Calvary.

The heading refers to a person having accepted Jesus as His own personal Saviour. Consequently, the divine nature, which is the nature of God, is instantly deposited in the believer (II Pet. 1:4). As well, at that time, the Holy Spirit also takes up residence within the child of God. It might be called the doctrine of "interpenetration." The idea is that we are in Christ, and Christ is in us.

Jesus said, *"At that day* (after the resurrection and the coming of the Holy Spirit on the Day of Pentecost) *you shall know that*

I am in My Father (speaks of deity; Jesus is God), *and you in Me* (has to do with our salvation by faith), *and I in you* (enables us to live a victorious life [Gal. 2:20; Rom. 6:3-5])" (Jn. 14:20).

THE BODY IS DEAD BECAUSE OF SIN

This speaks of the human body. Paul says it this way in order that the believer knows and understands that he must not try to gain victory over sin by means of his own physical body—self-will, personal efforts, one's own strength, etc.

The believer's human body is dead in the sense that it has death in it because of sin, which speaks of original sin—Adam's sin that brought forth spiritual and physical death to each member of the race. In view of that, and as Paul has already adequately explained, one's willpower alone which has to do with the human body, simply cannot bring about the needed results, but actually can only hinder what the Spirit of God alone can do.

So, Paul is saying that one is foolish to resort to these pitiful measures when he already has tremendous firepower, so to speak, within his heart and life in the form of Christ and the Holy Spirit in order to bring about what is needed.

BUT THE SPIRIT IS LIFE BECAUSE OF RIGHTEOUSNESS

Paul is speaking here of the Holy Spirit, which is obvious. He is God and as a result can do anything. In other words, He is almighty. So, one is not to think that his situation is so bad that the Holy Spirit is insufficient.

I remind the reader that this is the same Spirit of God who *"moved upon the face of the waters"* in Genesis 1:2. The earth at that time *"was without form, and void,"* and in six days' time the Holy Spirit brought it back to a habitable state, as well as created all animals, fowls, fish, and human beings.

Understanding that, I think that the Holy Spirit has the power to do whatever is necessary.

THE SPIRIT IS LIFE

The Holy Spirit has life and is actually, through Christ, the source of life. Man has no spiritual life within himself due to his spiritual death. Even the life that the believer has is that which is imparted by the Holy Spirit. So to attempt to bring life out of death (the physical body of the human being) is a futile effort.

All life is in the Spirit, and all life emanates from the Spirit. It is obtained by faith in Christ and what He did for humanity at Calvary and the resurrection. In other words, the Cross makes everything possible.

RIGHTEOUSNESS

The *"righteousness"* addressed here is the righteousness of God, which is given to any sinner upon faith in Christ, and it is given instantly.

Within himself, man has no righteousness, despite the fact that he attempts constantly to manufacture such, which the Bible calls self-righteousness (Lk. 18:9-14).

The righteousness of God is defined as "moral perfection." It is right because it is God's way; consequently, it is absolutely devoid of any type of wrongdoing. As well, it is the standard set by God and not by man. It is the only righteousness that God recognizes. As such, He is instantly angry at man's efforts at self-righteousness, which God calls wicked (Ps. 7:11; Rom. 1:18).

One might say that righteousness is simply that which is right; however, it is God's definition of what is right and not man's. Within himself, man has no righteousness, can have no righteousness, and, because of the fall, man is depraved. However, upon simple faith in Christ, the Lord imputes a perfect, unsullied, spotless righteousness called "the righteousness of God," which is made possible by the Cross and our faith in that finished work.

BUT IF THE SPIRIT OF HIM WHO RAISED UP JESUS FROM THE DEAD DWELL IN YOU...

"But if the Spirit of Him who raised up Jesus from the dead dwell in you, He who raised up Christ from the dead shall also quicken your mortal bodies by His Spirit who dwells in you" (Rom. 8:11).

The same power of the Holy Spirit that raised Jesus from the dead dwells in believers and is available for our use. This is what Paul is saying.

The idea is that there is no temptation or sin so black, so binding, or so destructive but that the Spirit of God can handle it, that is, if we know the truth respecting the finished work of Calvary. That same resurrecting power is available to all believers.

The same power that raised Christ from the dead is available to us, and that we must understand. To think of such power is beyond comprehension and amazing to realize that it is at our disposal.

However, for that power to be manifested on our behalf (and it is intended to be), the Holy Spirit demands one thing in particular, and that is that our faith be in the correct object. What is the correct object?

That which must be the object of our faith at all times is Christ and the Cross (Gal. 6:14; Col. 2:10-15; I Cor. 1:18; 2:2). The believer must understand that the Cross opened the door for the Lord to give us anything and everything that we need. It is so simply because all sin was atoned at the Cross, and I mean all sin—past, present, and future—at least for all who will believe (Jn. 3:16). Somehow most Christians seem to have a problem believing what I've just said, and above all, doing what I've just said, which is to anchor their faith in Christ and the Cross.

Why?

Perhaps the reasons are many, but I think the greatest reason of all comes twofold: First, it is unbelief, meaning that the believer simply does not believe what I've said about Christ, the Cross, and the Holy Spirit. Second, the Cross of Christ exposes all the efforts of man and makes them look foolish, which does not sit well with religion. In other words, it exposes the flesh.

HE WHO RAISED UP CHRIST FROM THE DEAD SHALL ALSO QUICKEN YOUR MORTAL BODIES BY HIS SPIRIT THAT DWELLS IN YOU

Many erroneously believe that Paul is speaking here of the coming resurrection. That is incorrect. By Paul using the word *mortal,* this means that he is speaking of our present experience in Christ. In other words, the Holy Spirit will impart whatever power is needed to our present physical bodies (mortal) in order that we may have victory in any and every capacity of life.

In the Greek, the word *quicken* is *zoopoieo,* and it means "to cause to live, make alive, give life." So He will infuse spiritual life into these physical bodies, which always takes precedence over the death that is already there due to Adam's fall.

Paul is dealing here not only with the fact of sin that we face every day in our physical bodies, but also in the fact of original sin, which is the cause of the problem in the first place.

The Holy Spirit imparts enough life into these physical bodies to overcome death and give us strength to say *yes* to Christ in whatever capacity that He requires.

Even though this of which we have stated is the thrust of Paul's statement, nevertheless he also in a secondary sense is speaking of the coming resurrection of life when the Holy Spirit will also at that time give every believer a glorified body (I Cor. 15:38, 51-57).

THEREFORE BRETHREN

"Therefore, brethren, we are debtors, not to the flesh, to live after the flesh" (Rom. 8:12).

If the believer will maintain his faith in Christ and the Cross, whatever else happens, the grace of God will continue to come to him in an uninterrupted flow. This provides the greatest life and living that man could ever know.

The two words, *"therefore brethren,"* portray the fact that Paul is addressing his statements to believers and not unbelievers, as should be obvious. Unbelievers have no interest in the Bible, do not care what it says, and really do not believe what it says. So the Bible is for believers. Concerning that the Scripture says, *"But the natural man receives not the things of the Spirit of God: For they are foolishness unto him: Neither can he know them, because they are spiritually discerned"* (I Cor. 2:14).

Actually, the entirety of the Bible all the way from Genesis 1:1 through Revelation 22:21, is the story of Jesus Christ and Him crucified.

Some expositors claim that the carnally minded and those who are in the flesh pertain to the unsaved. Not so! Paul is speaking to believers, hence him saying *"brethren."*

WE ARE DEBTORS

The heading refers to that which we owe the Lord Jesus Christ. In the Greek, the word *debtors* is *opheiletes,* and means "one held by an obligation," in this case, obligated to Christ.

It is our Lord who paid the price at Calvary's Cross, giving Himself as the perfect sacrifice in order that all sin would be atoned and that believers could walk in victory. We owe everything to Him. We do not owe anything to the world of religion or any other human being or philosophy, etc. We owe it all to Jesus, and the reason is simple. It is because He is the one who has paid the price.

NOT TO THE FLESH

The heading means that the believer does not owe anything in that direction, and in fact has done nothing but suffer from that means. We continue to speak of the flesh.

To be sure, Paul's statement, although directed to the subject at hand, covers far more territory than meets the eye. It has to do not only with this struggle between the flesh and the Spirit, but as well spreads out to include religious men who would attempt to force the believer to abide by their man-made religious laws. All of that is of the flesh just as much as anything else one could name.

The idea is that I, as a believer, do not owe anything to another Christian, even as Paul will later say, except to love him (Rom. 13:8). There Paul said, *"Owe no man anything,"* or, in other words, "I am not a debtor to any man to obey him in anything as far as believers are concerned, except to love him in Christ."

Consequently, this shoots down all religious, man-devised hierarchies.

TO LIVE AFTER THE FLESH

As a child of God, I must order my life after the Holy Spirit who will always guide me according to truth, i.e., the Word of God. As a believer, I owe the flesh nothing, and must not allow it to intrude in any part of my daily living before the Lord.

Sin is to no longer control me in any capacity because its dominion is broken. I am not to be guided by fleshly lusts or ungodly passionate desires. My hope alone is in Christ and what He did for me at the Cross. In Him I find all I need, and far more than I could ever need.

As a result, I do not guide my life after the conventional wisdom of the world, nor do I flow with its current. Its interests are not my interests. Its goals are not my goals. I am not moved by what moves it, nor do I respond to its appeal. There is a reason for all of that which Paul beautifully gives us in the next verse.

One other thing: For preachers who try to tell you to do things that you as a believer know is of the flesh, you do not owe them anything. In other words, don't do it, whatever it is. Please understand that if it's not faith in Christ and the Cross, irrespective as to what it might be or how religious it might sound, don't get involved. You don't owe such anything.

FOR IF YOU LIVE AFTER
THE FLESH, YOU SHALL DIE

"For if you live after the flesh, you shall die: But if you through the Spirit do mortify the deeds of the body, you shall live" (Rom. 8:13).

The unbelief of mankind is truly something that makes one marvel, especially considering the insurmountable proof otherwise. All goodness that proceeds from our flesh is rejected by God.

Once again, this has a far greater meaning than meets the eye. The thrust of the subject as it is given by Paul is that a person who lives habitually under the dominion of the evil nature (referring to believers) could ultimately lose his soul. Consequently, this shatters the unscriptural doctrine of unconditional eternal security.

Whenever the word *die* is used in this fashion, it actually refers to the final death in the lake of fire, which is one dying but never knowing the relief that death brings (Rev. 20:11-15).

This speaks of the believer who does not avail himself of what Christ did at Cavalry, therefore continuing to live habitually under the dominion of sin. God will always be patient, loving, longsuffering and compassionate, and He will forgive anytime and every time, irrespective of the sin or the frequency, if the person is truly sincere (I Jn. 1:9). Still, the danger is that the individual will begin to make allowances for his sin, quit seeking forgiveness, and lose his way totally.

No one can live with habitual sin without reaping its bitter results, irrespective of the forgiving grace of God. Sin always takes a deadly toll. In fact, it greatly weakens one's faith, and that is the great danger.

The only answer for sin, and I mean the only answer, is what Jesus did at Calvary in atoning for all sin, at least for all who will believe. If one wants to know how bad sin is, one only has to look at the Cross, and then one should say, "My sin did this."

THE WORLD'S SYSTEM

Paul's statement speaks, as well, of believers playing loose with the world, actually becoming a part of the world, i.e., living after the flesh. Even though Paul is not here and now address-ing this particular subject, the analogy nevertheless holds true. The world's system is antagonistic to the child of God. In other words, it is hostile to the believer's faith. That's the reason Paul said, *"Wherefore come out from among them, and be you separate, says the Lord, and touch not the unclean thing; and I will receive you"* (II Cor. 6:14-18; 7:1).

If there is not a separation from that system, as well, the believer who is constantly associating himself accordingly could ultimately die, i.e., lose one's soul.

BUT IF YOU THROUGH THE SPIRIT DO MORTIFY THE DEEDS OF THE BODY, YOU SHALL LIVE

First of all, one can only mortify the deeds of the body by and through the Holy Spirit. It cannot be done any other way. It is obvious here that Paul is speaking to believers because he is placing a choice before the believer. How in the world can an unsaved person expect anything of the Spirit of God when he doesn't even know the Spirit of God, and above all does not have the Spirit of God? No, Paul is speaking to believers, thereby warning believers.

We are told that it is only through the Spirit of God that we can overcome the sin nature. However, I remind the reader that this is done on the basis of the believer knowing and under-standing what Jesus has done for us at the Cross and our faith maintained in that finished work. If we leave out the Cross, we have in effect left out the Holy Spirit (Rom. 8:2).

THE CROSS OF CHRIST

Again we say even at the risk of being overly repetitive, that the presence of the Holy Spirit in the heart of the believer is potential in nature. His presence does not guarantee anything without the full cooperation of the believer. He has been sent to us to help, not to treat us as a slave (Jn. 16:7).

We are not to come to terms with the *"deeds of the body,"* i.e., the sin nature, but rather *"mortify them."*

In the Greek, the word *mortify* is *thanatoo,* and means "to kill; put to death." We are not to kill the body, but rather the deeds of the flesh which have their expression in the body, i.e., physical body.

This which Paul says is not a suggestion or a request, but rather an ultimatum. We destroy by the Spirit the effectiveness of the flesh, or it destroys us. Considering the results of not doing so—which is the loss of one's soul for all eternity—I think we should take these statements very seriously.

THE HOLY SPIRIT

If the Holy Spirit is given latitude, He will do these great things within our lives. Not only will He destroy the evil deeds of the body, as well He will also give the believer life, i.e., "you shall live."

It functions in this capacity: If the believer insists upon living after the flesh—allowing the flesh free course—then more and more sin will be added, with the situation ultimately becoming desperate. However, if the believer allows the Holy Spirit His complete latitude, more and more life will be the result, which in fact will never end. Death never stops while life, as well, never stops.

We must remember that we are speaking here of eternal things. As such, we should realize the seriousness of this that Paul is telling us.

One might say that if the believer does not kill sin, then sin will kill him. In effect, the believer cannot kill sin, but he has received a power that can make dead all the passions of sin in the body, and that is the power of the Holy Spirit, which is made available to us by and through the Cross of Christ.

FOR AS MANY AS ARE LED BY THE SPIRIT OF GOD

"For as many as are led by the Spirit of God, they are the sons of God" (Rom. 8:14).

Do you believe that the Cross of Christ is the only answer for sin?

Do you believe that the Holy Spirit works exclusively by and through the Cross of Christ?

The heading proclaims that which the Spirit wants to do. He wants to lead us according to the will of God. As such, He will lead us out of this domination by the sin nature, and lead us into total victory in Christ. That is where He has been instructed to lead us, and that is where He is leading us, providing we cooperate with Him.

One cannot be led by the Spirit of God unless his faith is exclusively in Christ and the Cross. This is a must! Considering that the Holy Spirit works entirely within the parameters of the finished work of Christ, and will not work outside of those parameters, it is incumbent upon us to place our faith exclusively in Christ and the Cross, and maintain it exclusively in Christ and the Cross. This is the only way in which one can be led by the Spirit of God. If we attempt this in any other way or manner, it will always and without exception lead to trouble.

THEY ARE THE SONS OF GOD

The phrase, *"They are the sons of God,"* pertains to what sons of God do—they are led by the Spirit of God.

In addressing the Corinthians, Paul said, *"You know that you were Gentiles, carried away unto these dumb idols, even as you were led"* (I Cor. 12:2).

As is obvious, he was speaking of the Corinthians before they gave their hearts to God. They were actually led at that time by demon spirits, but now they are led by the Spirit of God. Of course, the same is apropos for all believers and for all time.

There are so many privileges attached to being a follower of Christ that it is very difficult to properly enumerate them.

However, being led by the Spirit of God has to be one of the greatest attributes and blessings afforded the believer.

WHAT DOES IT MEAN TO BE LED BY THE SPIRIT OF GOD?

First of all, if one truly has Christ, i.e., is born again, at the same time, one has the Holy Spirit. It is impossible to be otherwise.

One cannot be united with Christ except through the Spirit (I Cor. 6:17); one cannot share Christ's Sonship without sharing the Holy Spirit (Rom. 8:14-17; Gal. 4:6); and one cannot be a member of the body of Christ except by being baptized into that body, and we aren't speaking of water baptism, but rather that which takes place at conversion (I Cor. 12:13; Rom. 6:1-5).

As stated, this is not a baptism into water, and neither is it a baptism into the Spirit, as the Scripture seems to indicate on the surface, but rather into the body of Christ (Rom. Chpt. 6). The body of Christ here is the element one is baptized into, which takes place, as stated, at conversion. The Holy Spirit is the agent who does the baptizing into the body. The believer is the candidate.

If it were the Spirit baptism (Acts 2:4), Christ would be the agent (Mat. 3:11). But at conversion the Holy Spirit is the agent, baptizing the believing sinner into Christ, which of course is not physical but rather spiritual (Jn. 3:6, 8). As such, the Spirit from above is the power affecting the new birth (Jn. 3:3-8; I Jn. 3:9), for the Spirit is the life giver (Jn. 6:63), like a river of living water flowing from Christ bringing life to him who comes and believes (Jn. 7:37-39). All of this is done—or one might say is able to be done—because of what Jesus did at the Cross.

THREE BAPTISMS

There are three baptisms in which every believer should be engaged:

1. The baptism into Christ. This takes place at conversion, and as we have just mentioned, it is not a physical thing, as should be obvious, but totally spiritual (Rom. 6:3-5).

2. The baptism into water (Mat. 28:19). Water baptism is an outward sign of an inward work that has already been accomplished. It does not save, and neither is it meant to save. It is meant to portray the fact that salvation has already been experienced.

3. The baptism with the Holy Spirit (Acts 2:4). As stated, at salvation the Holy Spirit in a sense baptizes the believing sinner into Christ. In the baptism with the Spirit, the Lord Jesus baptizes the believer into the Spirit (Mat. 3:11).

THE SPIRIT OF GOD AND DIVINE POWER

It is important to realize that for the first Christians in the early church, the Spirit was thought of in terms of divine power clearly manifested by its effects on the life and in the life of the recipient. The impact of the Spirit did not leave individuals or onlookers much doubt that a significant change had taken place in them by divine agency. Paul refers his readers back to their initial experience of the Holy Spirit again and again. For some it had been an overwhelming experience of God's love (Rom. 5:5); for others, joy (I Thess. 1:6); for others, illumination (II Cor. 3:14-17), for others, liberation (Rom. 8:2; II Cor. 3:17), for others, moral transformation (I Cor. 6:9-11), and for others, various spiritual gifts (I Cor. 1:4-7; Gal. 3:5).

Actually, in the book of Acts is the most regularly mentioned manifestations of the Spirit—the speaking with other tongues, prophecy and praise, and bold utterance of the Word of God (Acts 2:4; 4:8, 31; 10:46; 13:9-11; 19:6). Overall, speaking with other tongues is the initial physical evidence that one has been baptized with the Holy Spirit (Acts 2:4).

All of these things put together tell us why the possession of the Spirit as such can be singled out as the defining characteristic of the Christian (Rom. 8:9; I Jn. 3:24; 4:13), and why the question of Acts 19:2 could expect a straightforward answer (Gal. 3:2). The Holy Spirit as such might be invisible, but His presence is readily detectable (Jn. 3:8).

THE GIFT OF THE HOLY SPIRIT

The gift of the Holy Spirit was thus not simply a corollary or deduction drawn from baptism or laying on of hands, but a vivid event for the first Christians, and it continues to be such unto this hour. It is most probably the impact of this experience to which Paul refers directly in passages like I Corinthians 6:11, 12:13; II Corinthians 1:22, and Ephesians 1:13.

According to the book of Acts, the first Christians adapted their way of doing, their way of being, and their way of worship in accordance with the Spirit rather than vice versa (Acts 8:12-17; 10:44-48; 11:15-18; and 18:25-19:6).

THE SPIRIT AS THE POWER OF THE NEW LIFE

According to Paul, the gift of the Spirit is also a beginning that looks to final fulfillment (Gal. 3:3; Phil. 1:6), the beginning and first installment of a lifelong process of transformation into the image of Christ, which only achieves its end in the resurrection of the body that is yet to come (II Cor. 1:22, 3:18; 4:16-5:5; Eph. 1:13; II Thess. 2:13; I Pet. 1:2). The Spirit is the firstfruits of the harvest of resurrection whereby God begins to exercise His claim over the whole man (Rom. 8:11, 23; I Cor. 3:16; 6:19; 15:45-48; Gal. 5:16-23).

LIFE FOR THE BELIEVER

Life for the believer is therefore qualitatively different from what it was prior to faith. Our daily living becomes our means of responding to the Spirit's claim, enabled by the Spirit's power, which is what it means to be led by the Spirit (Rom. 8:4-6, 14; Gal. 5:16, 18, 25; 6:8). In other words, the Holy Spirit becomes the guide into all truth, the leader of everything, which is always toward Christ, and the final word concerning every decision in the life of the Christian, which is always according to the Word of God.

Actually, this was the decisive difference between Bible Christianity and Rabbinic Judaism for Paul. The Jew lived by law, the deposit of the Spirit's revelatory work in past generations. It was an attitude that led inevitably to inflexibility and a direct block to anything that God was now doing, since revelation from the past is not always immediately appropriate to the needs of the present. Regrettably this applies also to every single modern religious denomination that discounts the baptism with the Holy Spirit, claiming that all is received at conversion.

However, the Spirit of God brings an immediate, personal relationship with God, which actually fulfills all the great hopes of the past, and which makes worship and obedience something much freer, more vital, and more spontaneous than mere ritual (Rom. 2:28, 7:6, 8:2-4, 12:2; II Cor. 3:3, 6-8, 14-18; Eph. 2:18; Phil. 3:3).

A FINAL FULFILLMENT?

At the same time, because the Spirit is only a beginning of final salvation in this life, there can be no final fulfillment of His work in the believer as long as this life lasts. In other words, the Holy Spirit never really gets through with molding and making us into the image of Christ. The idea is that the man of the Spirit is no longer dependent on this world and its standards for his meaning and satisfaction, but he is still a man of human appetites and frailty, and part of human society.

Consequently, to have the Holy Spirit is to experience tension and conflict between the old life and the new, and between the flesh and the Spirit, exactly as we are studying here (Rom. 7:14-15; 8:10, 12; Gal. 5:16; Heb. 10:29).

Strangely enough, to those who saw the characteristic life of the Spirit in terms of visions, revelations, and the like, Paul replied that grace comes to its full expression only in and through weakness (Rom. 8:26; II Cor. 12:1-10).

However, in all things in which the Spirit leads us, and in all things that the Spirit does for us, we must never forget that the Holy Spirit is that person and power who bears witness of Christ—always to Christ and what He did for us at the Cross (Jn. 15:26; Acts 1:8; 5:32; Heb. 2:4; I Pet. 1:12; I Jn. 5:6-8; Rev. 19:10; I Cor. 1:17, 18, 23; 2:2; Gal. 6:14; Col. 2:10-15).

HIS OPERATION IN EVERY BELIEVER

A distinguishing feature of the Holy Spirit is that He is experienced by all and works through all, not just a select few (Acts 2:17; Rom. 8:9; I Cor. 12:7, 11; Heb. 6:4; I Jn. 2:20). We must also understand that the Holy Spirit works exclusively by and through the finished work (the Cross) of Christ. In fact, He will not work outside of those parameters. Before the Cross, the Holy Spirit could not abide in the hearts and lives of anyone except a few prophets, to help them carry out their work. When that work ended, He left. As far as believers were concerned, while the Holy Spirit was *with* them, He was not *in* them, and that is a vast difference.

Since Jesus paid the price on Calvary's Cross, thereby addressing all sin for the believing sinner, the Holy Spirit now instantly comes into the heart and life of every believer at conversion. Now don't mistake that for the baptism with the Spirit, for that's not what we're speaking of. What we are addressing is the Spirit of regeneration. This enables us to be saved.

As well, before the Cross, when believers died, they did not go into heaven, but rather down into paradise, where they were actually held captive by Satan. The Evil One could not hurt them, but their salvation and deliverance depended totally and completely upon the Cross. When Jesus died, thereby paying the price for all sin, Satan lost his ability to hold anyone captive who trusted in Christ, with them now becoming the captives of the Lord Jesus (Eph. 4:8).

Christ then led all of these pre-Cross saints out of paradise and into heaven itself. Since the Cross, when believers die, they instantly go to be with the Lord Jesus Christ in the portals of glory. In fact, the place that was once called paradise, which was in the heart of the earth, is now empty. It will probably be expanded into the lake of fire at the great white throne judgment.

Consequently, to have the work of the Holy Spirit in our hearts and lives on a continuing basis, which means 24/7, we must understand that the Holy Spirit works exclusively by and through the Cross of Christ (Rom. 8:2; Col. 2:10-15; I Cor. 1:17-18, 23; 2:2). In fact, we must be ever conscious of His manner of work. This means that our faith must be exclusively in Christ and the Cross, and I mean exclusively.

I was reading the other day behind a particular scholar, and he mentioned that every morning saints of God should pray that the Holy Spirit would have His way on that particular day, etc. While of course that's what we want, that's not really the way to obtain it.

We must place our faith exclusively in Christ and the Cross, and maintain it exclusively in Christ and the Cross, which then enables the Holy Spirit, who works exclusively within that domain, to work on our behalf, and to work grandly, and never stop working.

The great fault of the modern church is that it doesn't not know how the Holy Spirit works. They don't understand that He works exclusively by and through the Cross of Christ, and how does that work?

Before the Cross it was sin that hindered the Holy Spirit. Due to the fact that the blood of bulls and goats could not take away sins, the terrible fraction was still there, which greatly hindered the Holy Spirit. Since the Cross, which answered for all sin, the Holy Spirit now has free course. That is something we must understand.

THE CROSS OF CHRIST AND SIN

The believer must understand that the only place for sin is the Cross. This is the fault of the church: It keeps trying to address sin in all the wrong ways. That did not begin yesterday; it actually began at the dawn of time, when Cain and Abel offered up sacrifices. Cain offered up a sacrifice of the work and labor of his own hands, refusing to obey God to offer up a sacrifice of blood. His sacrifice was rejected. Abel offered a sacrifice that God demanded. For the situation did not address itself to how beautiful the sacrifice was, but what it represented.

When an innocent victim shed blood, which the lamb did as it was killed and put on the altar, Abel was saying that he was a sinner and needed a Saviour, of which the sacrifice was a symbol. God accepted it. Cain in essence was saying that he was not a sinner and did not need a Saviour. That is the problem of the church—offering up the wrong sacrifice. No doubt, the sacrifice of Cain was beautiful, and as a result millions today gather around the sacrifice of Cain, so to speak. The sacrifice of Abel was not beautiful, in fact it was ugly, revolting after a sense, seeing the little lamb slain, and consequently precious few are gathered around that sacrifice, but it is the sacrifice that God accepts.

I read where preachers tell people to fast for so many days and they will have victory over their problems. They won't. While fasting is scriptural—if it's done in the right way—it will not give one victory over sin. The Cross and the Cross alone gives victory over sin. In fact, every believer should, morning and night, state to the Lord that his faith and trust is in Him exclusively and what He did for us at the Cross, and not in ourselves or any other human being.

That's what Jesus was talking about when He said, *"If any man will come after Me, let him deny himself* (deny our own strength and ability), *and take up his cross daily* (please notice the daily), *and follow Me"* (Lk. 9:23).

Then Jesus said, *"And whosoever does not bear his cross and come after Me, cannot be My disciple"* (Lk. 14:27). So we are speaking here of something that is extremely significant, as I think would be obvious. Most believers have precious little help from the Holy Spirit because their faith is in something other than Christ and the Cross. Because it is so important, let me repeat myself and say it again.

The Holy Spirit works exclusively, and I mean exclusively through Christ and the Cross. In other words, what Jesus did at the Cross gives the Holy Spirit the legal means to do all that He does. Please read the following very carefully, and I quote verbatim from The Expositor's Study Bible:

For the law (that which we are about to give is a law of God, devised by the Godhead in eternity past [I Pet. 1:18-20]; this law, in fact, is 'God's prescribed order of victory') *of the Spirit* (Holy Spirit, i.e., 'the way the Spirit works') *of Life* (all life comes from Christ, but through the Holy Spirit [Jn. 16:13-14]) *in Christ Jesus* (any time Paul uses this term or one of its derivatives, he is, without fail, referring to what Christ did at the Cross, which makes this 'life' possible) *has made me free* (given me total victory) *from the law of sin and death"* (these are the two most powerful laws in the universe; 'the law of the Spirit of life in Christ Jesus' alone is stronger than the 'law of sin and death'; this means that if the believer attempts to live for God by any other manner other than faith in Christ and the Cross, he is doomed to failure) (Rom. 8:2).

SANCTIFICATION

What we have just described to you regarding how the Holy Spirit works is really the definition of sanctification. Once again, sanctification is a process which is extremely important, but which most of the modern church knows nothing about. If you were to ask most preachers what sanctification is, the answers would vary from A to Z.

Let us say it very clearly and plainly: Sanctification is the work of the Holy Spirit in the heart and life of the believer, bringing our condition up to our position in Christ. The moment the believing sinner comes to Christ, at that moment that believing sinner is fully and perfectly sanctified by the Lord. In fact, the Scripture says, *"And such were some of you* (before conversion)*: But you are washed* (refers to the blood of Jesus cleansing from all sin)*, but you are sanctified* (one's position in Christ)*, but you are justified* (declared not guilty) *in the name of the Lord Jesus* (refers to Christ and what He did at the Cross in order that we might be saved)*, and by the Spirit of our God* (proclaims the third person of the triune Godhead as the mechanic in this great work of grace)*"* (I Cor. 6:11).

Then once we are saved, we enter into what is referred to as progressive sanctification (I Thess. 5:23). This means that the Holy Spirit now begins to work in us, with us, by us and for us, bringing our condition, which is far below our position, up to that status. In fact, it is a lifelong project. The Holy Spirit is greatly hindered when our faith is in something other than Christ and the Cross. If one will notice as one studies the Word of God, the Holy Spirit never directs praise to Himself, but always to Christ. That is because Jesus is the one who paid the price at Calvary's Cross. In fact, faith in Christ and the Cross is the only faith that God will recognize. In the last 75 years, we have heard more about faith than all the balance of Christianity put together. Regrettably, almost all of it wrong.

Our faith must ever be in Christ and what He did for us at the Cross. That's not a one-time thing, but as I've already quoted you from Luke 9:23, it must be on a daily basis. This is the way the Holy Spirit works, and as previously stated, He will not work any other way.

To be sure, and thankfully so, the Holy Spirit does not desert us whenever we do wrong or we think wrong, etc. Still He is hindered greatly by our faith in that which He cannot honor.

This is the reason that the Cross of Christ is an offense (Gal. 5:11). The Cross of Christ lays waste all of man's efforts, no matter how noble they may be. This does not sit well with religious man. Anything other than the Cross always glorifies man's ability, which God can never accept. It is the Cross alone which glorifies Christ. That's the reason that Paul said, *"But God forbid that I should glory* (boast), *save in the Cross of our Lord Jesus Christ* (what the opponents of Paul sought to escape at the price of insincerity is the apostle's only basis of exultation), *by whom the world is crucified unto me, and I unto the world* (the only way we can overcome the world, and I mean the only way, is by placing our faith exclusively in the Cross of Christ and keeping it there, understanding this is the manner in which the Holy Spirit works)" (Gal. 6:14).

I am Thine, O Lord, I have heard Thy voice,
And it told Thy love to me;
But I long to rise in the arms of faith,
And be closer drawn to Thee.

Consecrate me now, to Thy service, Lord,
By the power of grace divine;
Let my soul look up with a steadfast hope,
And my will be lost in Thine.

Oh, the pure delight of a single hour
That before Thy throne I spend,
When I kneel in prayer, and with Thee, my God,
I commune as friend with friend.

There are depths of love that I cannot know
Till I cross the narrow sea;
There are heights of joy that I may not reach,
Till I rest in peace with Thee.

Draw me nearer, nearer, nearer blessed Lord,
To the cross where Thou hast died,
Draw me nearer, nearer, nearer blessed Lord,
To Thy precious, bleeding side.

How The
Holy Spirit
Works

SPIRIT OF
ADOPTION

SPIRIT OF ADOPTION

"FOR YOU HAVE NOT received the spirit of bondage again to fear; but you have received the spirit of adoption, whereby we cry, Abba, Father" (Rom. 8:15).

FOR YOU HAVE NOT RECEIVED THE SPIRIT OF BONDAGE AGAIN TO FEAR

An understanding of the message of the Cross dispels all fear. In fact, without a proper understanding of the Cross of Christ relative to sanctification, one is hard put to properly understand any of the great doctrines of the Bible, at least as they should understand them.

The *"spirit of bondage"* as Paul here uses the phrase, refers to the Old Mosaic law. The law demanded obedience, as all law demands obedience, and the person was a virtual slave to that process.

This does not mean that the law was bad, even as Paul has already addressed. Actually, he plainly said, *"The law is holy, and the commandment holy, and just, and good"* (Rom. 7:12).

However, the law, while good, still made its demands but gave no power to meet those demands. So Jews—at least those who tried to keep the law, even as they certainly should have—found themselves in bondage to that law, because it was something they simply could not do (the keeping of it) no matter how hard they tried. And yet they knew they must.

Any believer who presently embarks upon an effort of law-keeping, as possibly all of us have done in one way or the other, will find ourselves in that same bondage. I do not speak of the law of Moses presently quite so much as the laws, rules, and regulations made up by many churches. Nevertheless, it is law, with some of it probably very good.

Such efforts tend to fool people for the simple reason that many of these rules and regulations as stated are good, just as the law of Moses was good. Nevertheless, to reinstate law in any fashion, and no matter how sincere we may be, will not have the intended results of holiness, but rather the very opposite.

SO WHAT NOW WOULD CONSTITUTE LAW?

Any effort that we make—anything we do to try to gain victory over sin other than faith in Christ and what He did for us at the Cross, and faith alone in Christ and what He did for us at the Cross; anything else, everything else—is law.

For instance, it is being said that individuals can fast so many days, whether three, five, 21, etc., and thereby have victory over sin. While fasting is definitely scriptural, if it's done in the right way, but there is no way that sin can be overcome by fasting. The only place where sin can be addressed, defeated, and washed away is the Cross of Christ. Everything else is law, and God will not honor it.

This means that the poor soul who sets out to fast for 21 days and then does it will find his problem just as real when he concludes his fast as when he began. As someone has well said, after a while, we're going to have to eat, and then the problem comes back.

No, the Cross of Christ alone is the answer for sin. To be sure, sin is the problem, whether we want to admit it or not.

Incidentally, the recourse for Old Testament saints was always the sacrificial system which pointed to the coming Redeemer. It is the same presently, but with a fulfilled system— the Cross.

FEAR

Efforts at lawkeeping always bring fear for the simple reason that the person is led to believe that his salvation consists of keeping these laws, i.e., rules and regulations of his church, etc. So his Christianity now becomes a bondage instead of a free-dom—all in an attempt to be holy and righteous, which only Jesus can give. Actually, the believer cannot sanctify himself. It is not possible. As well, we are sanctified by what we believe far more than what we do. If we believe right, we will ultimately do right.

Lawkeeping can never give holiness or righteousness for the simple reason that the law was always broken.

The very moment that the believer attempts to keep law of some making, the Holy Spirit withdraws His help, and the believer always fails sooner or later. The idea is not in the believer keeping some type of law, but rather in placing his trust in Christ and what He has done for him at the Cross.

And to be sure, Christ has already kept the law in every respect, and He did it all for us. When we accepted Him, whenever that was, we were transferred immediately from the position of lawbreaker to the position of lawkeeper. It happened simply by our faith. It is a task already done instead of being left up to us to do, which no one ever did but Christ.

Some people have the mistaken idea when they read that of which we have just said that this means that believers have a license to sin. It is quite the contrary.

THE MORAL LAW OF GOD

In fact, the believer is definitely to keep every moral law of God. That's one of the great facets of Christianity—that our lives are changed from the evil and the ungodly to the righteous and the holy. However, this process cannot be brought about by lawkeeping on our part, but only by trusting in Christ and what Christ has done for us at the Cross.

Let us say it again: As the sacrificial system—the Cross—was the only hope for Old Testament saints, so is the Cross the only hope for New Testament saints.

As a result of our trust, Jesus keeps the moral law through us, which is in accordance with our imputed righteousness and holiness (Gal. 2:20). He does this through the power, agency, person, and ministry of the Holy Spirit within our lives (Rom. 8:2; I Cor. 1:17, 18, 23; 2:2; Col. 2:10-15).

Now there is no fear. The responsibility is not on my shoulders, but on Christ. As well, it is not that He will do these things, but in fact has already done these things. The bondage of religion is always spelled out in one word: Do. A true relationship with Christ is always spelled out in one word: Done.

BUT YOU HAVE RECEIVED
THE SPIRIT OF ADOPTION

If the believer has in fact, received the *"spirit of bondage,"* it was not given to him by the Holy Spirit, but rather by his church or that of his own making and doing. So the believer needs to look at his situation as to whether it matches up with this that Paul brings to us, or rather something else.

The heading proclaims the manner in which all believers are *"sons of God."*

In the Greek, the word *sons* is *huios,* and means "a mature child of God in a legal standing with God."

The believer is not to confuse the statement *"sons of God"* of verse 14, reflecting his status with that of Jesus, who is *"the Son of God."* We are such by adoption, while He is such as the only begotten Son of God (Jn. 3:16). John actually refers to Him in essence as the *"only begotten Son"* (Jn. 1:18).

The words *"only begotten"* do not only mean that our Lord was the only Son of God in this manner, but that He, as God the Son, is alone of His kind—unique, begotten of God through eternal generations. He is the image of God in the sense that He is a derived representation of God the Father, coexistent eternally with Him, and possessing the same essence, deity Himself. Being the only unique representative, He is also, therefore, the manifestation of God. He said to Philip, *"He who has seen Me has seen the Father"* (Jn. 14:9).

SONS OF GOD

Jesus is also the one who made peace through the blood of His Cross, meaning that He took away the enmity that was between God and man because of man's fall. That is, through His substitutionary death, He satisfied completely all the claims that the law of God had against us. As lost sinners, we violated that law. The justice of God demanded that the penalty—death—be paid. God in His love desired to save those who would come to Him in faith to appropriate salvation.

So, He in the person of His Son, Jesus of Nazareth, stepped down from His judgment throne to take upon Himself at Calvary your sin and mine and your penalty and mine. With God's law being satisfied, He is now free to righteously bestow mercy. Consequently, it is now possible for any sinner to be born again, and, as such, brought into the family of God by adoption, thereby, becoming a *"son of God."*

However, we should understand even as Paul tells us here, that adopted sons share the same rights and privileges as one born in the family.

Even though this great work was done by Jesus at Calvary, it is still the Holy Spirit who acts as the legal counsel to bring the believing sinner into the family of God.

When He does this, He is not bringing us into the position of slaves, which caused those under the law to shrink from God in fear because they had broken the law. Rather He is bringing us into the great family of God, which gives freedom and was purchased by Jesus Christ. As stated, this place and position is not one of fear, slavery, and bondage, but rather the very opposite. Jesus has kept the law in every respect, and upon faith in Him every believer is given the status as previously stated, of lawkeeper. In other words, the same status that Jesus now has.

ROMAN LAW

The Holy Spirit is the one who places the children of God as adult sons into a legal standing before God and in relation to Him.

Actually, what Paul is stating here, is a principle of Roman law that was prevalent in his day, and served as an excellent example contrary to Jewish law, which was somewhat different.

In Roman law, in the process of legal adoption, the chosen heir became entitled not only to the rights of the property, but also to the civil status. He inherited the burdens as well as the rights of the adopter; the adopted being made, as it were, the other self of the adopter—one with him.

As stated, this Roman principle of adoption was peculiar to the Romans. It was unknown to the Greeks and unknown by all appearance to the Jews, as it certainly is not found in the legislation of Moses, nor mentioned anywhere as a usage among the children of the covenant.

In essence, this tells us that the adopted son of God becomes, in a peculiar and intimate sense, one with the heavenly Father. What an honor! What a privilege!

WHEREBY WE CRY, ABBA, FATHER

The heading presents the status of the adopted believer. Slaves were never allowed to say "Abba" to a master or "Imma" to a mistress. The word *Abba* is a Syrian term which Paul translates in Greek to "the Father." Jesus used the term *Abba* in His Gethsemane prayer (Mk. 14:36) which Mark also translates into Greek.

However, Greek scholars say that the Greek word is not meant to be a mere translation of the Syriac, but that the name "Father" is repeated. Robertson says it is a child's privilege to repeat the name, in other words, "Abba, Father." The Holy Spirit enables the child of God to call God "Father," which is done so because of Jesus Christ.

In all of this Paul is telling us that the believer has received the power that can make dead all the passions of sin in the body. This is done through his knowledge of Christ and what Christ has done for him at the Cross, which then gives the Holy Spirit the ability to make real that knowledge within one's life. As stated, this is a work of the Holy Spirit, and tells us that we are sons of God. This glorious work does not put the believer under the bondage of law, where he would be perpetually oppressed with doubts and fears as to whether he was righteous before God, but it brings him into the high and glorious position of a child who, possessing his Father's nature, spontaneously cries out "Abba, Father."

In the Greek, the word *cry* is *krazo,* and means "a loud cry expressing deep emotion." In other words, it speaks of much more than mere title, but rather relationship.

The believer must understand that before the Cross, Jews never referred to God as their heavenly Father. They would have almost considered it to be blasphemy for one to do so. So when Jesus came, addressing God as His Father, they were taken aback, they were completely nonplussed. They actually considered that He was blaspheming.

Of course we know He was not blaspheming, God in fact was His Father. Since the Cross, any and every believer can refer to God as his heavenly Father, and in fact should do so. It's all made possible by the Cross. Before the Cross, not only the Jews, but no one else would refer to God as their Father. But now all of that has changed, and because Jesus atoned for all sin—past, present, and future—at the Cross. This made it all possible for everything to change. Now I am in Christ Jesus, and He is in me, and of course we are speaking spiritually. Now I can refer to God as my heavenly Father, the same as the Lord Jesus Christ.

Of course there is a vast difference in us and in Christ. God the Father is the Father of Christ, and is such by eternal generations. He is our Father inasmuch as we have been adopted into the family.

Paul said, *"And if children, then heirs; heirs of God, and joint-heirs with Christ"* (Rom. 8:17).

He also said, *"Wherefore you are no more a servant, but a son; and if a son, then an heir of God through Christ"* (Gal. 4:7).

Once again our position is all made possible by the Cross of Christ. That's at least one of the many reasons that Christ and the Cross must ever be the object of our faith.

THE SPIRIT ITSELF BEARS WITNESS WITH OUR SPIRIT

The phrase, *"the Spirit itself,"* should have been translated, *"the Spirit* Himself." The Holy Spirit is a person, and accordingly should never be addressed as "it."

The phrase, *"bears witness with our spirit,"* means that He is constantly speaking and witnessing to us a certain thing. It is more, much more, than a witness when we first were saved, but rather a continuing witness, something that never stops.

"Bears witness with," in the Greek is *summartureo,* and means "to bear joint witness with" some other person or "to bear joint-testimony with" some other person.

"Our spirit" refers to the saint's human spirit energized by the Holy Spirit. In other words, our own spirit tells us that we are God's children, but the voice with which it speaks is, as we know, prompted and inspired by the divine Spirit Himself.

Once again, this is all made possible by the Cross. Before the Cross, the Old Testament saints had no such witness. The reason was simple: The blood of bulls and goats could not take away sins, so the witness was not there. When Jesus died on the Cross, thereby atoning all sin—past, present, and future, at least for all who will believe—then the Holy Spirit took up abode within our hearts and lives at the moment of conversion, and thank God, He will never leave.

The mere fact of His constant presence tells us that we are saved, that every sin has been washed clean by the precious blood of Jesus Christ. Not only that which is most important, but the Holy Spirit also witnesses to us by leading us and guiding us into all truth—something which never ceases and never stops.

Before the Cross, the Holy Spirit was *with* believers, but since the Cross, the Holy Spirit is *in* believers. There is a vast difference. Once we begin to understand this, even a little bit, we begin to see the Cross of Christ and its vast significance. We see how that the Cross is the means by which all of these wonderful things are done with us, by us, for us, and of us.

THAT WE ARE THE CHILDREN OF GOD

The heading speaks of present tense, meaning that we are the children of God, *right now*.

What the Spirit witnesses to us is something far higher than the mere knowledge of a philosophy, or even a personal experience we may have had. While personal experiences in the Lord are of extreme importance and never to be demeaned, that is if they are scriptural, still the witness of the Spirit of which we speak, transcends all feelings and means that it is stamped in the legal standing of the Word of God. It is a certitude (for certain) of the Spirit's presence and work continually within us, which takes us not only from experience to experience, but from faith to faith. It is manifested in His comforting us, His stirring us to prayer, His reproof of our sins, and His drawing us toward works of love to bear testimony before the world. Olshausen said, "On this direct testimony of the Holy Spirit rests, ultimately, all the regenerate man's conviction respecting Christ and His work."

It is amazing that many in this modern climate claim that God no longer speaks to people presently. They should read Romans 8:16 where the infallible Word of God proclaims that the Spirit of God not only speaks to believers, but as well speaks constantly. Perhaps these doubters do not know of this truth, simply because He is not in their lives, i.e., they are not born again.

Once again, and at the risk of being overly repetitious, we must inform the reader that all of this—the Holy Spirit witnessing to us constantly—is made possible by the Cross of Christ. If you listen closely, He will constantly say that we are the children of God, and the Bible plainly tells us so.

AND IF CHILDREN, THEN HEIRS

"And if children, then heirs; heirs of God, and joint-heirs with Christ; if so be that we suffer with Him, that we may be also glorified together" (Rom. 8:17).

The biblical truth of the veracity of the Cross of Christ is so overwhelming as to be staggering. With that being the case, how can the Cross of Christ be rejected by those who claim Christ? The heading speaks of a present position. In other words, we are heirs at this very moment. The phrase, *"And if children, then heirs,"* speaks of a present position. In the Greek, the word *if* is *ei,* and it means "a fulfilled condition." It probably could be better translated, "and since children." In other words, the Spirit *right now* is constantly bearing testimony *right now,* in company with our spirit *right now,* that we are children of God *right now.*

This means that we don't have to wait until some distant, appointed time; rather we are saved at this very moment, in fact, as saved as we ever will be.

As we've already stated, we are made *"heirs of God, and joint-heirs with Christ"* all because of the Cross of Christ.

Never forget that.

Never stop talking about that.

Never place that in an elementary position.

It's the Cross, the Cross, the Cross!

HEIRS OF GOD

The heading speaks of this adoption as being the highest of all, not merely a secondary position, even as glorious as that would be. This is illustrated in the story given by Jesus of the prodigal son.

THE PRODIGAL

The prodigal, so sick of his lost condition with all of its attendant misery, was planning on going back to the father and requesting of him, *"Make me as one of your hired servants"* (Lk. 15:19).

The hired servant did not even have the status of a regular servant who had full security and employment, but rather one who stood at the gate every morning and took whatever work was available, irrespective of its servility or shortness of duration.

However, when he came back to the father, he found that the father did not treat him as a servant, much less a hired servant, but brought him back to full status as a son, with all of its full inheritance, even though the previous inheritance had been squandered. This is what Paul is talking about when he says, *"heirs of God."*

Adam squandered the inheritance given to him by the Lord, and now guilty, his sons come back to the Father and are received not as servants, but as sons with all the privileges that the Father can give. In other words, total status and position are restored, with all rights reinstated.

If one is to notice, there was no condemnation whatsoever on the part of the father as regarding the prodigal son, but rather the very opposite. Hence Paul would say, *"There is therefore now no condemnation to them which are in Christ Jesus, who walk not after the flesh, but after the Spirit"* (Rom. 8:1).

Let me say it again: the Cross of Christ made possible all of this. Because of the Cross, I am at this present time an heir of God and a joint-heir with the Lord Jesus Christ. What a position! What an honor! And all made possible by the Cross.

AND JOINT-HEIRS WITH CHRIST

The heading means that we could never have this relationship with the Father, were it not for the last Adam—the Lord

Jesus Christ. He, as our representative man, has done for us what we could not do for ourselves, and at tremendous price, one might quickly add. So, this privilege and position of being a joint-heir with Him is strictly because of what He did at the Cross of Calvary. His mercy, grace, love, and compassion— and not at all through anything that we have done—gives us this place and position. Simple faith in Him grants me all the privileges that He has with the Father, which makes me an heir of God.

Roman law made all children including adopted ones equal inheritors, which Paul no doubt had in mind.

By contrast, Jewish law gave a double portion to the eldest son. However, Paul is saying that Jewish law (the law of Moses) does not apply here, because grace lifts one to a higher status, and therefore gives us equal rights with Christ.

As one reads these words, one is humbled, especially considering the price that was paid, and how much none of us deserve any of this that the Lord so freely gives.

Jesus is the eldest Son, but He has purposely forfeited His place and position of the double portion, rather making all believers equal with Himself regarding inheritance.

One can only shout, *Hallelujah!*

IF SO BE THAT WE SUFFER WITH HIM

Does the heading mean that we have to get on a Cross and thereby suffer with Him, so to speak? No. Paul is speaking of that which took place in our lives when we were born again.

We literally entered into His suffering on the Cross when we accepted Him as Saviour. Paul said:

> Do you not know, that so many of us as were baptized into Jesus Christ were baptized into His death? Therefore we are buried with Him by baptism into death: That like as Christ was raised up from the dead by the glory of the Father, even so we also should walk in newness of life. For if we have been planted together in the likeness of His death, we shall be also in the likeness of His resurrection (Rom. 6:3-5).

We reap that what He suffered for. Millions of Christians have gotten it into their minds that if they are good Christians, they will suffer in some way. They consider that to be holiness or righteousness. It isn't. When we do such a thing as that, we are in essence saying that what Jesus did at the Cross, in other words His great suffering there, was not enough, and we need to add something to it. That is an insult of the highest order. When Jesus said, "It is finished," that covered everything.

I reap that. I benefit from that which He has suffered. Even though the Cross of Christ was the most horrible thing that one can imagine, and yet it made possible every good and wonderful thing that I have today—all because of what Jesus did at the Cross. Please understand, if you do not know what it really means to suffer with Him, then you don't understand the Cross.

In regard to this, Jesus also said, "If any man will come after Me, let him deny himself (deny his own strength and ability), and take up the Cross daily, and follow Me" (Lk. 9:23).

Most Christians read that and pass over it quickly, because they think that Jesus is talking about suffering. He is, but it's not our suffering, it's His. He suffered that we might have all the wonderful things that we now have. That's what Paul is addressing here.

Jesus Christ is the source of all things we receive from God, but the Cross of Christ is the means by which all these wonderful things are made possible to us. I have it because He suffered greatly that it might be mine.

Please don't think that the Holy Spirit is telling us that we've got to enter into some type of physical suffering and think that's the Cross we have to bear. Rather, the Cross of Christ is the greatest fount of blessing the world has ever known, and ever will know.

THE CHURCH

In 1997, when the Lord began to open up to me the Message of the Cross and how the Holy Spirit works, I was elated, to say the least. In my mind, I thought that the church—and I speak of the worldwide church—would be so thrilled and happy to hear this tremendous truth. To my dismay, I found that they were not interested. Even beyond that, I found that the problem not only was ignorance, but unbelief as well, which is far worse. In other words, they simply didn't believe that the Cross of Christ is the means by which all of the wonderful things from the Lord are given to us.

At the present time, strong religious denominations that once held for the truth of the gospel, have become so shot through with unbelief that they no longer even remotely resemble what they once were. While there are some in these organizations who still cling to the straight gate and the narrow way, for the most part, the leadership is not in that category. A situation, I might quickly add, that is going to continue to deteriorate.

One could easily speak of modern psychology which is wholly unbiblical and in fact anti-biblical, with virtually all of Christendom having plunged into this pit. The truth is that psychology, which is the religion of humanism, is but a symptom of the real problem. The real problem is a failure to follow the Word of God, either because of self-will or unbelief, or both. Such mirrors perfectly the spiritual condition of the Israel of Jesus' day.

Israel had never been more religious than at the time of the first advent of Christ. But that was their problem—mere religion with no relationship at all with God. Consequently, they murdered their Messiah, and, in spirit, such continues to be done even unto this very hour.

CAIN

The problem is not new. At the very dawn of time, Cain murdered his brother, Abel. God approved of Abel's sacrifice while disapproving that of Cain. Consequently, Cain murdered his brother, and that spirit has continued unto this very hour. That's what I mean by the apostate church (Gen. 4:3-9).

It must be understood that if the sacrifice was accepted, this meant that the one (Abel) offering the sacrifice was accepted, whomever he may have been. If the sacrifice was rejected, as it was with Cain, this means that the one offering the sacrifice (in this case, Cain) was at the same time rejected.

Joseph's suffering (even as Abel's) was from his brethren. David's great enemy was Saul and certain elements in Israel. It was Israel who killed its own prophets and not the heathen. It was the church of Jesus' day that crucified Him and not actually heathenistic Rome. It was apostasy that gradually weakened the early church until finally, the world was plunged into the Dark Ages. Regrettably, it continues into the present. And, due to the deception of these last days, it will only grow worse, even ushering in, at a point in time, the Antichrist.

THAT WE MAY BE ALSO GLORIFIED TOGETHER

The heading pertains to the coming resurrection of life when every true saint will be glorified exactly as Christ is now.

The idea is that if one is a true believer—and please understand that this number is not nearly as large as one would think—he is going to be opposed by the false way, which is actually one of the great signs of the true way of the Word of God. Jesus suffered the opposition of the apostate church of His day, and all others suffer accordingly—that is if they truly know the Lord.

As this heading proclaims, that is beside the point. When the trump sounds, all of that is going to be forgotten, and rightly so. We are now sanctified, and we are now justified, and we will be glorified.

WHAT DOES IT MEAN TO BE GLORIFIED?

As stated, this pertains to the coming resurrection.

We can possibly best answer the question by addressing ourselves to three questions:

1. What do we know of resurrection as transformation?
2. What do we know about the resurrection state?
3. What is resurrection power?

THE RESURRECTION AS TRANSFORMATION

John wrote that God has made us His own children and then added, *"and it doth not yet appear what we shall be: but we know that, when He (Jesus) shall appear, we shall be like Him"* (I Jn. 3:2).

In I Thessalonians 4:14, Paul provides the broad outline of the resurrection when Jesus returns. He is speaking of the rapture—or resurrection—both words refer to the same event.

He spoke of those who had died in the faith. In other words, their souls and spirits going to be with Jesus, and then will come back with Him in the resurrection. This has to do with that large group receiving glorified bodies. This will include every saint of God who has ever lived—dead and alive—with all the sainted dead being reunited with their souls and spirits. All, both those who are dead and those who are now alive, will be instantly glorified and will meet the Lord in the air (I Thess. 4:13–18).

There are more details in I Corinthians 15 to these questions: How are the dead raised? With what kind of body will they come? (I Cor. 15:35). Paul simply notes that the resurrection body will correspond to our present bodies, but in contrast, it will be imperishable, glorious, and infused with power—spiritual rather than natural. It will be in the likeness of Jesus through a transformation that will happen *"in the twinkling of an eye, at the last trump."* Then the *"dead shall be raised incorruptible, and we shall all be changed"* (I Cor. 15:35–52).

THE RESURRECTION STATE

What do we know about the resurrection state? We know very little according to the apostles Paul and John.

However, many have found it fascinating to observe the capabilities of the resurrected Jesus and they speculate what being *"like Him"* might mean.

For instance, the resurrected Jesus had flesh and bones (Lk. 24:39). Why not flesh and blood? It is because *"the life of the flesh is in the blood"* (Lev. 17:11). The resurrected person is infused with a different kind of life.

The truth is, whereas the blood was that which formerly contained the life of the human body, now it will be the Holy Spirit.

Others have noted Jesus' sudden appearance among His disciples in a locked room (Jn. 20:26). Is this teleportation? Or can a resurrected person move between the atoms of the physical universe?

While all the questions are not now answered, this we do know: The limitations of our physical nature will then be gone, and whereas we are now perishable, we will then be imperishable. Power will replace weakness to such an extent as to be beyond present comprehension. As well, immortality (eternal life) will end mortality (death). In other words, there will be no more dying as it regards the resurrected saints.

WHAT IS RESURRECTION POWER?

This is one of the most exciting of New Testament themes. Paul writes, *"If the Spirit of Him who raised Jesus from the dead dwell* (is living) *in you, He who raised Christ from the dead shall also quicken* (will also give life to) *your mortal bodies by* (through) *His Spirit, who dwells* (lives) *in you"* (Rom. 8:11).

The point Paul makes is that the Holy Spirit—the agent of Jesus' resurrection—lives within the believer. It is the doctrine, one might say, of interpenetration. This means that resurrection power is available to us even in our mortal bodies, at least to a certain degree. Through the Holy Spirit, we are raised beyond our human limitations and enabled to live a righteous life, and as well, to do the works of Christ—all because of the Cross (Jn. 14:12).

Actually, this doctrine is sometimes overlooked and certain biblical passages are therefore, misinterpreted.

For instance, in Philippians 3, Paul is not expressing uncertainty about his own resurrection when he yearns to somehow *"attain unto the resurrection of the dead"* (Phil. 3:11).

The sentence reads, *"That I may know Him* (I want to know Christ), *and the power of His resurrection, and the fellowship of His sufferings* (the benefits of His sufferings), *being made conformable unto His death* (trusting in His death): *If by any means*

I might attain unto the resurrection of the dead (walk in newness of life.)" (Phil. 3:10-11).

RESURRECTION POWER NOW!

Actually, Paul's thought is focused on the present—living a resurrection kind of life *now*—not on eternity. He is expressing the desire (even that which he definitely experienced) the power of Jesus' resurrection would be at work in our lives presently to help us live a holy life. In other words, he wants the same power that raised Jesus from the dead to work in us now, which it will if we *"suffer with Him,"* i.e., look to the Cross with Him.

It is the will of God for every believer to live the resurrection life, which can only be done by the believer placing his faith exclusively in Christ and the Cross, and maintaining it exclusively in Christ and the Cross. The Cross of Christ is the means by which all of these wonderful things are made possible to us.

Paul also said, *"For if we have been planted together in the likeness of His death, we shall also be in the likeness of His resurrection"* (Rom. 6:5).

This plainly tells us that if we are to have resurrection life now, which enables us to live a holy life—victorious over the world, the flesh, and the Devil—then we must first be planted in the likeness of His death, which means to have that for which He died.

So, we hear certain individuals talk about the resurrection life, but they ignore the Cross or even reject the Cross. Please let it be understood that there is no resurrection life, in fact, there is nothing from God without the Cross. The Cross of Christ is the means, as stated, that opens the door for all of the wonderful things that God desires to give us.

As I'm sure should be obvious, when we talk about the Cross, we are not speaking of the wooden beam on which Jesus died, but rather what He there accomplished.

THE DOCTRINE OF RESURRECTION AND CHANGE

The Greeks thought the soul had permanent existence and that it possibly had renewed life through transmigration (to pass at death from one body or being to another—a form of reincarnation). However, they did not believe that the soul was the individual's conscious personality. Neither did they believe that this new state was a resurrection. Resurrection was, in fact, so foreign to Greek thought as to be considered ridiculous. The idea was, Why would anyone want to go through all of this all over again? Of course, they had no knowledge of what true resurrection actually meant.

THE JEWS

In the Jewish world of the first century, opinion was divided. The Orthodox Pharisees were confident of a resurrection, but the Sadducees denied the doctrine. This division was possibly brought about by the lack of clear teaching in the Old Testament concerning this great doctrine. However, while the teaching was not extensive, it was very clear in what little it did say (Job 14:14; Ps. 17:15; 49:7–20; 73:23–26; Isa. 25:8; 26:19; Dan. 12:2).

THE RESURRECTION OF JESUS

It is the New Testament that makes God's plan for individual human beings clear. There is an eternal destiny—a life beyond this life and, incidentally, life that will not end. Resurrection lies ahead. Jesus' own appeals to the Old Testament show evidence sometimes overlooked, but it is the resurrection of Jesus that is the final proof. Jesus' resurrection not only declared Him to be what He claimed to be—the Son of God—but also provided a guarantee for us who believe. Because Jesus lives, we too will live. We will share His destiny, which is actually what we are studying in Romans 8:17.

It must ever be understood that had not Calvary accomplished its intended purpose, which was to atone for all sin, there could not have been a resurrection because the Bible says that the "wages of sin is death." Consequently, Calvary was not dependent on the resurrection, but rather the resurrection was totally dependent on Calvary.

FOR I RECKON THAT THE SUFFERINGS
OF THIS PRESENT TIME

"For I reckon that the sufferings of this present time are not worthy to be compared with the glory which shall be revealed in us" (Rom. 8:18).

The emphasis of our redemption and resurrection must always be on the Cross. Unfortunately, the emphasis is a multitude of other things as it regards the modern church.

The heading speaks of the misery and ruin into which man and the creation are fallen because of man's sin, and we speak of the fall in the garden of Eden.

In the Greek, the word *reckon* is *logizomai,* and it means "to compute; to calculate." The word implies reasoning: I judge after the calculation is made. The word refers to a process of reasoning which results in the arriving at a conclusion. When Paul used the words "present time," he was speaking not only of his particular day, but also of a condition that has existed ever since the fall and will exist until the second coming of the Lord. The salvation of this world is the second coming of the Lord. To be sure, it is not one of several answers, but actually the *only* answer.

The following should be noted:

- The rapture of the church will save the church. Were it not for the rapture, I'm afraid that apostasy would ultimately destroy the church.
- The second coming will save the world. If that is not to be realized, then the world would destroy itself. It would have to, because sin can only steal, kill, and destroy.

ARE NOT WORTHY TO BE COMPARED WITH THE GLORY WHICH SHALL BE REVEALED IN US

The future time for which man and the creation hope is the promised day of the coming resurrection, when the redeemed and the creation will be delivered from the bondage of mortality and brought into the freedom of immortality. The glory of that future time will bear no relation to the misery of this present time.

The words *"shall be revealed in us,"* in the Greek text carry the idea of "toward us and upon us." In other words, it will be a reflected glory, reflected from our Lord in His glory, which will make the saints radiant when they return to the earth with the Lord Jesus at the second advent.

FOR THE EARNEST EXPECTATION OF THE CREATURE

"For the earnest expectation of the creature waits for the mani-festation of the sons of God" (Rom. 8:19).

The heading would have been better translated, "For the earnest expectation of the creation."

In the Greek, *Earnest expectation* is *apokaradokia,* and means "a watching with the head erect and outstretched." Creation speaks of everything, both animate (refers to that which has conscious life such as human beings and animals) and inani-mate (speaks of that which does not have conscious life, such as plants, trees, etc.).

WAITS FOR THE MANIFESTATION OF THE SONS OF GOD

The heading pertains to the coming resurrection of life. The idea is that due to the fall everything is cursed (Gen. 3:17).

According to Psalm 8, inasmuch that God has put the entirety of His creation under the dominion of Adam, it seems like the entirety of the creation, including outer space, also suffered the result of the fall. Consequently, nothing works as it should work and because of this curse.

As well, in some mysterious way, even as the Holy Spirit through the apostle here proclaims, the whole of creation both animate and inanimate, waits in suspense for the coming resurrection.

In other words, the creation presently is not functioning as it was originally created—note the storms, hurricanes, famines, etc. It cannot do so until the Creator returns and makes everything right, which He definitely will.

In the Greek, the word *waits* is *apodechomai,* and it means "assiduously and patiently to wait for."

MANIFESTATION

In essence, this tells us that all of creation is involved in some way in the fortunes of humanity. However, if creation be personified, this naturally leads to the idea of a mysterious sympathy between the world and man, and this is what the apostle expresses. He is saying, or at least the Holy Spirit is saying this through him, that creation is not inert, utterly unspiritual, and alien to our life and its hopes, but rather the natural ally of our souls because of being created by God.

In the Greek, the word *manifestation* is *apokalupsis,* and means "an uncovering; a laying bare." That is, the non-rational creation, subject to the curse put upon it because of man's sin, is expectantly waiting for the glorification of the saints that it also may be delivered from the curse under which it now exists. Inasmuch as man was given dominion over all of God's creation (Ps. 8), then everything was subject to the curse.

SONS OF GOD

The phrase *"sons of God"* speaks of all believers, even as Paul said in Romans 8:14, and are such because of what was done by the last Adam at Calvary and the resurrection. The first Adam brought on the curse, with the last Adam paying the price for deliverance from the curse. Soon, the curse in its totality will be lifted when Jesus returns.

However, this manifestation will come in two parts:

At the moment of the resurrection (I Thess. 4:16–17), all saints who have ever lived will be glorified. However, inasmuch as Jesus will not return to this earth at that particular time, total manifestation will not be brought about. That awaits some years later, which will be after the great tribulation. This will bring Israel back to God, which will occur at the second coming (Zech. Chpts. 13–14; Rev. Chpt. 19). For the manifestation to be complete, the Jews must also return to the Lord, which they will.

Then the curse will be lifted totally and completely from all things, with Christ reigning supremely on this earth and in person, and in a sense forever (Isa. 2:1–5; 4:2–6; 9:6–10; 14:1–8; 25:6–12; 26:1–4; 32:1–15; 33:6; 63:1–19).

THE CROSS OF CHRIST

Just about every fad of which one could think has been adopted by the church. One might say, anything except the Cross of Christ.

Even though we have given the following already in this volume, due to its vast significance, please allow the repetition:

- Jesus Christ is the source of all things we receive from God (Jn. 1:1-3, 9-10, 14; 14:6; 1:29).
- The Cross of Christ is the means, and the only means, by which all of these wonderful things are given to us (I Cor. 1:17-18, 23; 2:2).
- With Jesus as the source and the Cross as the means, the Cross of Christ must ever be the object of our faith. This is critical inasmuch as God will recognize no other type of faith (Rom. 6:1-5; II Cor. 13:5; Col. 2:10-15).
- With Christ as our source, the Cross of Christ as the means, and the Cross of Christ ever the object of our faith, then the Holy Spirit, who works exclusively within the framework of the finished work of Christ, will work mightily on our behalf, giving us victory over the world, the flesh, and the Devil, and helping us to grow in grace and the knowledge of the Lord (Rom. 6:1-14; 8:1-11).

I've seen the lightning flashing, I've heard the thunder roll,
I've felt sin's breakers dashing, trying to conquer my soul,
I've heard the voice of my Savior, telling me still to fight on,
He promised never to leave me, never to leave me alone.

The world's fierce winds are blowing, temptation sharp and keen,
I feel a peace in knowing, my Savior stands between—
He stands to shield me from danger when earthly friends are gone,
He promised never to leave me, never to leave me alone.

When in affection's valley, I tread the road of care,
My Savior helps me to carry my cross I am privileged to bear,
My feet, entangled with briars, ready to cast me down,
My Savior whispers His promise: I will never leave you alone.

He died for me on the mountain, for me they pierced His side,
For me He opened that fountain, the crimson, cleansing tide,
For me He's waiting in glory, seated upon His throne,
He promised never to leave me, never to leave me alone.

How The Holy Spirit Works

CHAPTER 6

HOPE

HOPE

"FOR THE CREATURE WAS made subject to vanity, not willingly, but by reason of him who has subjected the same in hope" (Rom. 8:20).

FOR THE CREATURE (CREATION) WAS MADE SUBJECT TO VANITY

We now only have a part of what the Cross of Christ has afforded. At the resurrection, the full complement of what the Cross has purchased will be available to all believers.

As stated, the heading pertains to the fact that inasmuch as God gave Adam dominion over all His creation, Adam's fall signaled its fall as well. As the creation *"was made subject"* to Adam, it was also subject to his sin, which resulted in a curse on all things.

In the Greek, the word *vanity* is *mataois,* and means "idle, resultless, futile, and aimless." In other words—empty nothings.

It describes something that does not measure up to that for which it is intended.

Here the creation is viewed as originally created—a perfect creation to glorify God. When the curse was put upon it, that purpose was interfered with in that a perishing and decaying creation cannot perfectly glorify Him. It was rendered relatively futile in that respect.

As we have stated, in some mysterious way, it seems that it is not fulfilling its intended purpose.

NOT WILLINGLY

The words of the heading mean that creation did not sin, even as such cannot sin, and therefore, had no part in the reason for the fall. However, inasmuch as Adam had dominion over all, all fell with him, including the whole of the human family.

In fact, due to the fall, which has terribly and adversely affected all of the creation, man has absolutely no idea what it originally was before the fall. Considering how beautiful that creation is presently, which speaks of the animals and plant life, as well as the heavens, I wonder as to exactly how beautiful and glorious it was before the curse of sin perverted its true purpose.

However, what the first Adam lost, the last Adam—the Lord Jesus Christ—has redeemed with all (at least believers and the creation) eagerly awaiting His return. As the song says, "Our Lord is coming back to earth again!"

BUT BY REASON OF HIM WHO HAS SUBJECTED THE SAME IN HOPE

The heading speaks of God as the one who passed sentence. The expositors say that Paul did not use the grammatical form which would express the direct agency of God, but rather that it was done *"by Him who has subjected."* In other words, it was done on account of Him. The idea is that God had stated that if Adam disobeyed, judgment would come, which is exactly what happened. It could probably be said to be the law of sowing and reaping (Gal. 6:7). It was not so much that God directly did the thing (effected the destruction), but rather that He said that it would happen, in essence because of certain laws which He had originally instituted. Consequently, it was Adam's sin and not God's will that was the direct and special cause of the subjection to vanity. The supreme will of God is thus removed "to a wider distance from corruption and vanity."

The words *"in hope"* state that the sentence of man, however, was not hopeless, and creation shares in his hope as in his doom. When the curse is completely removed from man, as it will be when the sons of God are revealed, it will pass from creation also, which will take place in the coming kingdom age. For this creation sighs.

Creation was made subject to vanity on the footing of this hope. The hope is latent, so to speak, in the constitution of nature as it only can be, and comes out in its sighing in some manner, to a sympathetic ear, which is exactly that of the Lord.

BECAUSE THE CREATURE ITSELF
ALSO SHALL BE DELIVERED

"Because the creature itself also shall be delivered from the bondage of corruption into the glorious liberty of the children of God" (Rom. 8:21).

The heading presents the direction of this hope. The hope is that of the subjected (creation) not the subjector (God). Nature possesses in the feeling of her unmerited suffering, a sort of presentment of her future deliverance.

However, the words *"shall be delivered"* in this phrase tell us what type of hope is being addressed here. The word *hope,* as is normally used, presently contains no certitude; however, that which the Holy Spirit uses through the apostle speaks of a guaranteed positive conclusion, but not exactly known when. If one is to notice, Paul did not say "the creature itself hopes to be delivered," but rather, *"shall be delivered,"* which speaks of that which is certain.

FROM THE BONDAGE OF CORRUPTION

The heading speaks of mortality, i.e., death. In the Greek, the word *corruption* is *phthora,* and means "moral corruption, decay, ruin, depravity, wickedness." It also speaks of that which is "perishing and being destroyed," which is the application for creation, in this case, mostly inanimate, but can include the animate, i.e., animals, fowls, fish, etc.

The idea is not that animals will live forever in that coming time, but that they will function as God originally intended, which speaks of their nature being changed to that of docility (Isa. 11:6–9).

INTO THE GLORIOUS LIBERTY OF
THE CHILDREN OF GOD

The heading expresses the mysterious sympathy that we have mentioned between the creation and man. When man fell, creation fell. When man shall be delivered, creation will be delivered as well, and is expressed in the word *also*.

"Glorious liberty" can be translated "the liberty of the glory." It refers to the glory of verse 18.

Then redeemed man will be as he was before the fall, but with one great difference: Redeemed man will be glorified, which is far greater than what Adam previously had. That's the reason it is called *"glorious."* The idea is, *"Where sin abounded, grace did much more abound"* (Rom. 5:20).

FOR WE KNOW THAT THE WHOLE CREATION

"For we know that the whole creation groans and travails in pain together until now" (Rom. 8:22).

It means exactly what it says—every single thing created by God, and all things created were created by Him (Jn. 1:3).

Evolution has all kinds of hypotheses, but they do not know the first cause. In other words, how did everything begin? Some evolutionists will say, "Well, it began with a cold cloud." Another will say, "Well, it began with a hot mist." But the question is, where did that come from? Of course the Bible gives us the beginning of all things, the first cause, *"In the beginning God"* (Gen. 1:1).

GROANS AND TRAVAILS IN PAIN TOGETHER UNTIL NOW

The heading refers to the common longing of all the elements of the creation, not to its longing in common with God's children.

In the Greek, the word *groans* is *sustenazo,* and it means "to experience a common calamity," which in this case refers to the fall.

In the Greek, the word *travails* is *sunodino,* and it means "pangs in company with or simultaneously." However, travail is different from groans in that the travail carries with it an expectation of relief from suffering.

This does not speak of the entirety of creation. It is readily understandable concerning the inanimate creation, as well as believers who truly know the Lord and are cognizant of the reason for man's present difficulties. However, it does not explain the unsaved of humanity who make up the far, far greater majority. One might argue that the word *together* does not include them, but it does.

The unsaved groan, but for an entirely different reason. The believer groans because he knows the cause of so much suffering (sin) and the only deliverance, which is the coming of the Lord. The unbeliever groans under the weight of rebellion against God, and the misery it brings, but never quite knowing the reason.

The believer travails but with the expectation of deliverance, while the unbeliever does the same—but deliverance from the wrong source, which in reality, is no deliverance at all.

NOT ONLY THEY, BUT OURSELVES ALSO

"And not only they, but ourselves also, which have the firstfruits of the Spirit, even we ourselves groan within ourselves, waiting for the adoption, to wit, the redemption of our body" (Rom. 8:23).

What Jesus did at the Cross will ultimately reconcile all things. One can say, as well, without the Cross, the reconciliation could never be. This means that everything looks backward to the Cross (past tense), and everything presently looks to the Cross (present tense).

The heading picks up on believers, with Paul giving a greater explanation, and for the simple reason that it is believers only, as we have stated, who know the true state of affairs. Believers know that Jesus is coming, that is if they truly know the Bible. They also know that He is the answer to all things, hence, all true believers say with John the Beloved, *"Even so, come, Lord Jesus"* (Rev. 22:20). Men can form their united nations and their conclaves, and they can claim to solve the problems of humanity, but it is a fruitless task. The situation will not be resolved, will not be answered, will not be rectified, and will not be made right until the second coming of the Lord when He—King of kings and Lord of lords— will rectify all things. And He most definitely shall!

WHICH HAVE THE FIRSTFRUITS OF THE SPIRIT

The heading tells us that even though believers presently have the Holy Spirit, still all that He can do and all that He will do will only be carried out and brought about at the coming resurrection. In other words, we only have a small portion now of what Jesus did at the Cross of Calvary, with the full import awaiting the trump of God.

The Holy Spirit is God. That means He is almighty, meaning He can do anything. As well, He is omniscient, meaning that He knows all things—past, present, and future. He is also omnipresent, meaning everywhere. However, due to certain particulars, as we have stated, we now only have the firstfruits, or the beginning of all for which Jesus paid such a price at Calvary's Cross.

The word *firstfruits* means a portion, or one might say, a down payment. When our Lord comes back, then the Holy Spirit will be given full latitude to do what needs to be done to bring everything into proper focus. As stated, that will not take place until the first resurrection of life.

EVEN WE OURSELVES GROAN WITHIN OURSELVES

The heading tells us, in essence, that all Jesus paid for and accomplished in the atonement at Calvary's Cross has not yet been realized and will not be fully realized until the resurrection of life. While in the body, believers are not yet exempt from their share in the universal groaning. In effect, believers presently have *"the earnest* (or the down payment) *of the Spirit"* (II Cor. 1:22), which means as stated, a down payment of all that He will yet do. As well, we now only have *"the earnest of our inheritance"* (Eph. 1:14), which speaks of only a partial payment, with the full payment, as stated, yet to come.

This answers many questions, or at least it should, concerning the reason for much Christian suffering. Unfortunately, some modern Bible teachers have attempted to consider all present suffering and difficulties as a lack of faith. While a lack of faith definitely does play a part in many things concerning believers, there is still no amount of faith that can bring the blessing of the coming resurrection into the present.

WAITING FOR THE ADOPTION

The heading could be translated, "waiting for the fulfillment of the process, which adoption into the family of God guarantees."

The idea is that even though we, as believers, have already been adopted into the family of God, which means that God is our heavenly Father, and Jesus is our elder brother, we still do not even remotely have all that this adoption process guarantees. It is coming, and it will take place at the resurrection of life.

TO WIT, THE REDEMPTION OF OUR BODY

This tells us that our physical body has not yet been redeemed. The link which unites the believer with the suffering creation is his body. Because of sin, it is subjected to pain, decay, and ultimately to death, and we speak of original sin. This connection with the creation brings a heart that is indwelt by the love of Christ into conscious suffering. It is the suffering of sympathy.

The sense of the pain and evil that encompass the creation oppresses the believer. The more conscious we are of the indwelling warmth, liberty, and power of the divine nature, which is love, the more we are sensible of the weight of the misery introduced into the creation by sin. In other words, we know that sin is the cause of all the problems. We also know that the Cross of Christ is the only answer for sin. We grieve when we see the modern church ignore the Cross, consequently adopting fads which not only carry forth no positive result, but also leads one astray.

The believer is united to the creation by his physical body and to heaven by the Holy Spirit, and the sympathy that we feel for the suffering creation is a divine sympathy. As believers, we know that things aren't right.

In other words, hurricanes are not the will of God. Famines and earthquakes aren't the will of God. All of that is because of the fall. As believers, we know what it could be and what it will be when Jesus comes back, but for now we suffer with the creation.

Because of man's sin, God subjected the creation to death, even as verse 20 proclaims, but He did so in hope. We look forward to its recovery when man shall be fully redeemed, and then all for which Jesus paid such a price will be ours in totality.

IS HEALING IN THE ATONEMENT?

The answer to the question is most definitely yes!

Every single thing that man has lost because of the fall was addressed in the atonement, i.e., the Cross of Calvary. Admittedly, we do not have all of this yet, actually having only a down payment, but everything, and I mean everything, was most definitely in the atonement.

The word *atonement* means "a making at one" and points to a process of bringing those who are estranged into a unity. Its use in theology is to denote the work of Christ in dealing with the problem posed by the sin of man, and in bringing sinners into right relationship with God, which was done at Calvary's Cross.

In this, Jesus dealt with the sin question and all of its effects. That means that the terrible sin debt was paid—it was no longer held against man, at least those who believe in Christ and what He did for us at the Cross (Jn. 3:16).

In dealing with the sin question, which Jesus did in totality by offering up His pure, spotless, sinless body as a sin offering at Calvary, He settled the sin question and its effects once and for all (Isa. Chpt. 53). The effects speak of sickness, poverty, ignorance, and slavery. So, that means that healing is definitely in the atonement, as well as prosperity, etc.

THE WILL OF GOD

That means it is the will of God and always the will of God to save from all sin, heal from all sickness, redeem from all poverty, deliver from all bondage and spiritually educate from all ignorance.

Yet we know that despite this great thing which Jesus did at Calvary, at times, Christians still sin, the sick are not always healed, prosperity is not the offing for all, and some spiritual bondages are not broken, at least not quickly.

Why?

The answer is obvious. Even as Paul has so plainly said, believers presently only have the firstfruits of the Spirit, which means all that Jesus did at Calvary has not yet come to the believer, and in fact, will not come in totality until the coming resurrection. However, that doesn't mean that believers should live in a type of spiritual apathy and saying, "Whatever will be, will be." Many things can now be changed and are in fact changed constantly by believers believing God and having faith in who He is and what He can do. So the believer is to believe God for whatever is needed, irrespective that we now only have the firstfruits.

Yet, at the same time, preachers should not claim that the failure of many of these things can be explained by a lack of faith. That, as should be painfully obvious, is unscriptural. In other words, all the people I pray for aren't healed, but I still believe that God heals. To be frank, any and every believer in the world, and I mean those truly dedicated to the Lord, if they do certain things, they can have their lives improved and drastically so.

What are those things?

- In the first place, every believer should place his faith completely and totally in Christ and what Christ has done at the Cross, understanding that the Cross of Christ is the means for all things that we receive from God. This is imperative. Our faith must not be in ourselves, must not be in other people, but rather in Christ and what He did at the Cross, and it must be maintained accordingly.

- Second, the believer should have a protracted prayer life. In other words, every single day, seven days a week, we should get alone with the Lord, even if it's only 15 or 20 minutes, and thank Him for all the things that He has done, and then tell Him what we would like to have, of course if it's in His will. One would be surprised as to how quickly He will answer such a prayer.

- We must then exercise faith in what we have asked Him to do, thereby believing that He is able, and that He wants to help us. Again, we must continue with our faith in Christ and the Cross.

- If a believer will do this without fail, he will see his life change for the better in every direction. It may take a while for it to come to pass, but it will come to pass, and I speak of those things for which he has importuned the Lord.

THE MODERN FAITH MESSAGE

The following material has been previously printed in one of our commentaries, but due to the manner in which commentaries are normally studied and the significance of this subject,

I feel it is proper to reprint this article at this time. As well, there is some repetition in the material, but which we think is necessary in order to properly develop the correct emphasis.

As well, some of the following material was authored by someone else, but I have no way of ascertaining the identification.

I feel like there are many elements in the modern faith teaching which are positive. Much of it is wholesome, edifying, and needful. Emphasizing faith certainly does tend to elevate victorious Christian living, and this is definitely essential within the body of Christ.

If the "faith teaching" stopped there, it would be of untold value to the work of God—but regrettably, much of it does not stop there. Sad to say, because of error, many individuals participating in this teaching have not been led to victory but rather defeat, and complete defeat at that. In fact, many have quit living for God and many have died all because of this false teaching.

To the unlearned—those unfamiliar with the Word of God—it sounds logical, scriptural, and inviting. This, of course, is why it ensnares so many people. Much error rides into the church on the back of truth.

The following lists some of the errors that I believe permeates the modern faith teaching:

- *Bibliolatry.* What we mean by bibliolatry is that words of Scripture seem to be deified—apart from the living God—and collected into various "laws" which activate the forces of good and evil. Anyone who questions the specific interpretations is immediately branded as "denying the Word of God and its power." One could say that the sin of bibliolatry is committed. This occurs when one makes an idol of the Bible or has excessive reverence for the letter of the Bible, in this case claiming that repeating certain passages over and over bring certain forces into play, etc. As such, the Bible itself, apart from Christ we may quickly add, is looked at as the source. This is idolatry just as surely as is the bowing down to heathenistic idols. However, it is very subtle and therefore, far more dangerous because of its religious context.

- *Knowledge.* Knowledge is said to be the way to achieve a divine place in creation. Attainment of "a new-creature status for the believer" makes them part of a superior, elite, or master race, they teach. This fits right in with the political message in the Christianizing of the culture and ultimately leading the world into the millennium. Just as with the ancient error of old called Gnosticism, a superior knowledge is claimed. Consequently, whether the advocates realize it or not, knowledge becomes the way to salvation instead of Christ.

- *Confession.* The confession principle is strictly adhered to, which teaches that the use of scriptural formulas to "confess" results releases the forces of good on one's behalf, they say. Again whether they realize it or not, the advocates of the confession principle are taking control out of the hands of the Lord and placing it into their own hands. In other words, they automatically conclude that they know the will of God in any and all circumstances, which of course is ludicrous. The conclusion of that is to ultimately attempt to use the Word of God against God, which is against His will, and which, of course, the Lord will never allow to be done. For instance, when the three Hebrew children were facing the fiery furnace, they exclaimed that the Lord was able to deliver them. However, they went on to say, *"But if not, be it known unto you, O king, that we will not serve your gods, nor worship the golden image which you have set up"* (Dan. 3:17–18). *"But if not,"* would have been considered a bad confession by the so-called faith people, but God did not call it such.

- *Law.* They teach that all sin is a consequence of the law, which disappeared with the new covenant, and that confession of sin becomes a false perception because behavior is made right (they say) by confessing "who one is in Christ Jesus." Repentance then plays no part in our present-day experiences, in their thinking, because it relates to sin—which ended with the law. As a result of this teaching, any preaching that convicts of sin is called condemnation and rejected out of hand. Actually, they little believe in Holy Spirit conviction, claiming that it represents a throwback to condemnation which ended with the abolishment of the law (the law of Moses). Any confession of sin is pretty much denied because it is a "wrong confession" of who one is in Christ. As a result, one of the great office works of the

Holy Spirit—His convicting of *"sin, and of righteousness, and of judgment"*—is denied or erroneously interpreted (Jn. 16:8–11).

- *Confession of sin.* For instance, they claim that John 16:8-11 pertains only to the world and not to the believer. However, the word *world* simply means that it applies not only to the Jews, but also to Gentiles, in other words, to all people. John also said, *"And He is the propitiation for our sins: And not for ours only, but also for the sins of the whole world"* (I Jn. 2:2). Basically this teaching claims that sin, conviction of the Holy Spirit, repentance, etc., belong to the old covenant (law) and have no validity under the new covenant. Therefore, they have an erroneous conception of what sin is and its cure, which is Christ and the Cross. They actually teach that when a Christian sins, he should not acknowledge it, should not mention it, and, above all, should not confess it to the Lord, but rather confess that he is the righteousness of God, etc. They claim that the first chapter of I John is written only to the unsaved, and not to believers. The reason? This particular chapter completely obliterates their thinking and their belief system. John plainly said, *"If we confess our sins, He is faithful and just to forgive us our sins, and to cleanse us from all unrighteousness"* (I Jn. 1:9). There is no way that one can properly exegete this particular Scripture, or any part of the first chapter of I John and come to the conclusion that it is for unbelievers only and not Christians. Such thinking is ridiculous.

THE SIN NATURE

The Word of Faith people, which I do not believe is faith at all, at least that God will accept, basically deny human nature, claiming that the Christian is either divine or satanic, which is dualism. In other words, they deny the sin nature, which goes along with their erroneous understanding of "New Creationism."

Consequently, the struggle between the flesh and the Spirit, which characterizes the life of every Christian, is pretty much denied as well. "How can there be a struggle if one is a new creation?" they claim.

In answer to that theory, John the Beloved wrote, *"If we say that we have no sin* (sin nature)*, we deceive ourselves, and the truth is not in us"* (I Jn. 1:8).

SCIENTISM

Much modern faith teaching espouses a form of Scientism, teaching that laws and formulas can control circumstances around us.

This harks back to point one—the deification of Scripture— and points to "the superior knowledge." Everything is then judged on the so-called amount of faith that one has. When a person fails, as he always does, he is instantly labeled as not having faith as he should have had. Consequently, he is written off with a wave of the hand as being insignificant.

When one of their gurus suffers defeat as it regards sickness, or whatever, they simply try to ignore it as though it never happened. To be frank, that's all they can do, because fail they will.

THE CROSS

The Word of Faith people deny the Cross of Christ, claiming that it is the biggest defeat in human history, and that it is "past miseries."

This means that the Cross of Christ is not looked at in any way as a source of victory, being replaced by "proper confession." In their idea, the Cross plays no part in anything that pertains to the Lord. The victory, they claim, is attained by the resurrection.

Consequently any and all songs about the blood of Christ or the Cross are labeled as elementary and have little place in New Creationism.

They show a lack of knowledge of the atonement of Christ and what was accomplished both at Calvary as the source and key to all present victory. In effect, this is the most dangerous part of their teaching because anything that demeans Calvary in any way or relegates it to a secondary position is tantamount to spiritual suicide.

While it certainly is true that Calvary would have been of no effect without the resurrection, it was not the resurrection but Calvary that redeemed man from sin and all of its consequences. The Cross of Christ did not depend on the resurrection. Rather, the resurrection depended upon the Cross. If Jesus did all that He set out to do at the Cross, which was to atone for all sin, then the resurrection was guaranteed. If He had failed to atone for even one sin, He could not have been raised from the dead.

THE APOSTLE PAUL

This is the reason that Paul said, *"For I determined not to know anything among you, save Jesus Christ, and Him crucified"* (I Cor. 2:2).

Paul, who was no doubt the greatest Bible scholar of his day, made this statement for purpose and reason:

- That which Paul said about Calvary was what the Holy Spirit demanded.
- By experience, Paul knew that Jesus satisfied the sin debt at Calvary and there broke the power of the dominion of sin in the heart and life of the believer.

The only thing that stands between man and eternal hell is the Cross of Christ. When the church goes beyond Calvary, that's when the church loses its way. In fact, every single thing comes through Calvary: Salvation, the baptism with the Holy Spirit, divine healing, miracles, overcoming victory, answered prayer, prosperity, communion with the Lord, eternal life, etc.

Whether the present-day faith teachers realize it or not, their interpretation of the atonement is not consistent at all with the tenor of teaching throughout the Word of God. This lies at the very heart of this teaching, and it strikes at the very core of Christian belief.

If one gets everything right except the Cross, then everything is wrong.

SCRIPTURE

One of the basic teachings of this element is that all Scripture is not the same. In other words, some Scriptures pertain particularly (they say) to those who are still in the realm of the senses (flesh)—those who are sadly unenlightened. Some even go so far as to say that the apostle Paul demonstrated great lack of enlightenment in many of his experiences. And I Corinthians 4 is considered an example of this. Actually, they say the same thing concerning all of the apostles in the days of the early church.

In other words, these teachers say that if the apostles of old had the knowledge that the modern faith teachers possess today, they would not have been required to suffer many—if any—of the difficulties that they experienced.

In practice, only certain Scriptures are used by the faith teachers to support their contentions. Their basic difficulty with the Word of God is that they separate the Word from the person of the Lord Jesus Christ. In short, they have replaced God with their chosen Scriptures, rationalizing that this will justify their actions. Consequently, certain words of Scripture are deified—apart from the Living God—and exalted into various laws that bring the forces of good and evil into action.

They call themselves for the most part "Word" people, constantly quoting particular Scriptures, and thereby convincing the public that they are very scriptural and spiritual, thus making their contentions trustworthy.

In truth, they actually deny parts of the Bible as revelation not illuminated with a higher knowledge.

THE OLD TESTAMENT

Even though they call themselves "Word" people, they rely on only a few selected scriptural texts, actually taking them out of scriptural context. Consequently, they have very little respect for the Old Testament, seemingly suggesting that since Old Testament personalities did not have the written Word (or at least very much of it), they did not know very much. As a result, "Word" people only use isolated texts from the Old Testament in their teaching. They seem to completely ignore the fact that the entire framework of New Testament context (thought) is derived from Old Testament revelation.

Actually, one cannot arrive at a proper understanding of the New Testament unless he has a proper understanding of the Old Testament.

As someone has well said, the Old Testament is the New Testament concealed, while the New Testament is the Old Testament revealed.

Years ago, I heard a preacher make the statement that some individuals today worship the Bible apart from God, who inspired it. At first his statement puzzled me, but after some thought I feel that I understand what he was saying.

OUT OF CONTEXT

Basically he was suggesting that certain Scriptures, such as Mark 11:24 or John 15:7, etc., are taken out of context, used in some manner as a type of magic talisman (a good luck piece).

CHAPTER SIX **HOPE** | **175**

In other words, he was saying that particular Scriptures are taken completely out of context and used to deal with situations, even though they have almost nothing to do with the present difficulty at hand. These Scriptures are quoted over and over again, with the individual using them as a sort of club to force God or circumstances to line up with the person's reasoning.

Also, many of them insist that Scriptures that do not line up with their way of teaching are just simply not relevant today. Again, we emphasize their contention that if individuals such as the apostle Paul had possessed their scriptural knowledge, he would not have had to suffer persecution and trials. What a crock!

They go on to tout their experience in the Word, meaning that they are more "developed" than the apostles or prophets of old.

In truth, most of these teachers know very little about correct exegesis (interpretation) of Scripture—all the while proclaiming themselves to be "Word" people.

SUPERIORITY

As well, there is an air of superiority about these teachers, their teaching, and their followers. They are the "new creation" people. They have "the knowledge."

Of course, even with a superficial investigation, this is absolutely opposed to the teachings of the Lord Jesus Christ. Humility was the Master's great hallmark. One of His last acts on earth was the washing of the disciples' feet. Superiority and lack of humility are always of Satan; these never come from God. They reveal the worldling, the ego of man—believers in the so-called "master race."

They teach that one will continue to be a part of the "master race" unless one slips into using information from the "sense world."

As a member of this superior mold (or master race), one is made to feel that he is entitled to all types of riches and rewards; hence, the hundredfold return gospel. These teachers do not seem to realize that to demand a hundredfold return from God on our investment is to again turn the temple of God into a den of thieves, which is pretty well what it has become, at least in many circles.

THE GREED MESSAGE

The so-called hundredfold return gospel intertwined with a master-race theory has little or nothing to do with the love of God. It has little or nothing to do with the desire to promote God's cause or to give to Him simply because we love Him.

At best it is an investment or better yet a gamble. At worse, it is a deception perpetrated by Satan. At its core, it is little better than the Las Vegas practice of enticing people into gambling casinos with the selfish lure of something for nothing. Actually, I personally feel that the same evil spirit that promotes casino gambling, or any type of gambling, is the same spirit that characterizes the "greed gospel." This is the greed message so prevalent today.

These teachers hold the thought before their followers that their faith (or knowledge) will deliver anything they desire. Consequently, they must drive the largest cars, live in the finest houses, wear the best clothes, the best jewelry, and so forth. This is an image they must maintain. It is somehow supposed to demonstrate their faith. They are, in effect, role models for their followers.

As a result of this practice, the followers tend to look to the make of car, style of clothes, etc., as the mark of an individual's faith.

Some time ago, I heard one of their preachers preach on the subject of "K-Mart faith." His conclusion was that any Christian who shopped at such a place evidently had little faith.

To be frank, I did not hear the entire message because such drivel is so insulting to even elementary Scriptural intelligence that one can only stand so much.

CO-DIVINITY

This teaching claims that man is basically victorious through his knowledge rather than through Christ. It elevates him beyond his basic position as merely mortal. In essence, He becomes co-divinity with his Creator, or, in other words, a "little Jesus."

This satisfies two perverted needs in fallen mankind:

1. The need to be one's own god, in control of all of life.
2. The need to glorify oneself beyond one's proper place in creation, which is what caused the fall in the garden of Eden to begin with.

These teachers frequently use words like "dummies" or "idiots" to characterize those who do not believe in their particular way. This of course is a demonstration of one of man's basic problems today: ego. Man wants to play God. In actuality, he wants to be God. This is (and always was) Satan's problem too, and he has inoculated mankind with his desire for God-man equality.

Satan tempted Christ to misuse the knowledge and power of God when he suggested that Jesus create bread out of stones. The Lord gave Satan the correct reply, but this same desire—to misuse knowledge—is prevalent today.

They suggest as stated, that there was a basic lack of knowledge of the laws of healing and salvation until Paul's time. Consequently, Old Testament saints (according to these teachers) underwent many unnecessary difficulties because of this lack of knowledge. Of course, this is absurd, but it is their excuse for any Scripture which conflicts with their misguided teaching.

Actually, there is a tendency to emphasize knowledge rather than salvation. It is as though one becomes saved, then becomes more saved as his knowledge increases. It comes very close to ignoring the blood atonement of the Lord Jesus Christ, and actually does in some cases. In fact, one of their leading gurus plainly stated in one of his written messages, "The blood of Jesus Christ does not atone." Pure and simple, that is blasphemy.

THE WILL OF GOD AND THE WORD OF GOD

In their deification of superior knowledge, they seem to have lost the realization that true Christian belief is that the will of the

Father and the words of the Bible are in perfect conformity; they give life to us as we move in the knowledge of God according to the leading of the Holy Spirit, not in the bondage of a written formula that is separated and apart from our living Saviour.

When God's written Word is apart from His person, a scriptural code of law is developed. As with any code of law, legalism must develop—and with it the resultant condemnation whenever the believer fails to keep one or several of the laws.

If one would notice, faith teachers are often heard saying, "It was your faith that failed. God can never fail." Consequently, the believer becomes the one following the formula of faith to its maximum and taking the blame for any ensuing failure. According to them, the "faith law" or "formula" always works. The only possibility of failure, therefore, lies in our faith as revealed in our confession of the words or formulas. Of course, God never fails, and His Word never fails either; however, we must go back to the thought that we are living in a fallen world. We only have the firstfruits of the Spirit now, but with the totality coming at the first resurrection of life. Consequently, we don't have everything now, and will not have everything until the trump sounds.

LAWS

In view of this, they say we should lean on our knowledge which will then control all circumstances around us. These laws or formulas, by their actions, are impersonal and divorced from any relationship except that of their mechanical performance.

In fact, they say that these laws and formulas will work for the unsaved just as they will work for believers. How ridiculous!

By and large and as stated, this knowledge removes the control from God and His will to an exercise of our will, using the formula (or law). The line between God and man blurs, and man suddenly seems to become a law unto himself. Of course, this totally ignores the fact that Jesus, although He was the very Son of God, totally submitted Himself to the will of the Father. It would seem prudent for us to do likewise.

KNOWLEDGE SALVATION

This "knowledge salvation" imposes a great burden on the believer. He mustn't, under any circumstances, "lose his confession." If he does, all the results of the forces put into motion with the confession will be lost. One of their teachers said, "Action on the written Word of God brings God onto the scene."

It would seem from this teaching that God is automatically stirred into action by repetition of certain words of Scripture. Consequently, the believer acts solely upon the substance of his own faith world—guided by specific laws, confessions, and formulas.

THE LAW OF CONFESSION

Following hard on the heels of "knowledge" is "confession." Confession constitutes a major element in this so-called faith ministry.

Scriptural formulas confessing results into existence, thereby releasing benevolent forces on our behalf constitute a major force in this so-called gospel. Their "law of confession" is a routine quoting of certain Scriptures, and quoting them over and over. The Word of God is seen as a self-energizing entity—a deity within itself.

Specific Scriptures are utilized out of context most of the time, completely ignoring the related Scriptures addressing the same principles, which of course is a violation of proper Scriptural interpretation.

By using these isolated Scriptures, God is supposedly obligated to perform certain actions. The verbalized confession becomes the total force.

Of course, within this system the burden on the individual becomes almost too great to bear. Above all, he must not lose his confession; he must not weaken his confession; he must not err in his confession. No matter what happens, he is compelled to ignore reality and to maintain his confession. As a result, sick people are prayed for and automatically declared healed.

Why?

Once the confession has been made, and because certain specific passages of Scripture have been applied to their sickness, it is impossible for them not to be healed. In their thinking, the Word of God—which again has become a deity within itself— has been imprisoned within their laws and the individual has to be healed.

In these matters, the will of God, as well as all related circumstances, are totally ignored. The unfortunate individuals who find themselves under these teachers are at times instructed not to see a doctor since this would counteract their positive confession, with the consequent loss of their healing. The sad fact is that some have actually died by observing this dangerous and hurtful teaching.

JESUS AND THE WORD

As stated, the Word of God is basically removed from the person of the Lord Jesus Christ. Individuals are told that they can do anything Jesus did—if they have the right type of knowledge, believe correctly, and have the right confession; they can have anything they confess.

They are told that the believer, infused with a new kind of nature (the new knowledge), can speak (even as God spoke) worlds into existence. This type of teaching is often termed "the God-kind of faith."

Too often this teaching denies the effect of sickness, death, trials, and problems in their lives when these problems are present. They seem to feel that they have the power to release *"forces of good"* as a consequence of their knowledge and confession. As such, they have little compassion on those who are sick or who suffer from trials or difficulties. They simply state with a cold, scientific logic, "You are suffering because you have refused to know your place in Christ" (superior knowledge).

They also say that if you pray according to God's written Word and follow His instructions, you will always get results. If you miss it (they say), it is your faith that failed, not God.

They imply somewhat that prayer, in the sense of need, is the enemy of confession. They say that such prayer asks for help without denying that the circumstances exist; in other words, it is the opposite of confession. They suggest that rather than praying, we confess the answer, because in confessing the answer, we repeat the magic formula causing the negative factors to disappear.

PRAYER

They further imply that prayer (asking God for help) is a sign of weakness and dependence, so we should religiously avoid this type of praying.

Instead, they say we should confess our position in Christ because confession has the ready answer, and all we really have to do is begin confessing.

In view of this, we are instructed not to pray as one normally would, since prayer, as indulged by most Christians is really an enemy of faith, they say. Prayer is talked about, but in reality there is very little praying in these circles, with what they refer to as prayer—little more than words twisted to conform to the principle of confession.

Once again, the veil of condemnation falls heavily on the shoulders of the believer who is trapped in these false directions. He is told that he can govern the circumstances around himself, using only the written Word of God. He can use this as a club to force God into a particular position or at least as a magic talisman that will banish all problems.

RESPONSIBILITY

Trusting believers are further told that results probably will not happen overnight just because we "confess" certain things once or twice. In other words, we must keep saying them over and over again and keep believing them.

Once again, the responsibility of the results falls entirely on the individual. Consequently, the individual is the one who is glorified if and when results occur. The name of God and His Word are spoken of constantly and are "used" continuously. In actuality it is the individual who is glorified, and God receives very little of the praise. They even tell us that these are the same principles "used" by Jesus.

The believer, as stated, is discouraged from the usual manner of praying since this would require him to repeat the problem allowed for all to hear. This amounts to an acknowledgment of the problem which is a bad confession, they say. Some insist that praying for help implies that God has left something undone, that redemption is incomplete. Within this teaching, nothing is considered incomplete.

REPENTANCE AND FORGIVENESS

We are even told, at least by some of these teachers, that the prayer of repentance and forgiveness is not for the modern-day saint, and that no Christian should ever confess sin as one generally does. Some teach that a confession of sin should be replaced by a confession of who the believer is—a new creation in Christ. This is somehow supposed to erase the slip into sin consciousness.

If one would notice, these preachers or teachers seldom preach against any kind of sin. There is little said about it because (they say) it will cause people to have a sin consciousness. So the way not to sin is simply to ignore it, they say. As stated, and because it is so very important, we repeat it: They really do not believe in Holy Spirit conviction either. They suggest that conviction is really condemnation, which completely ignores John 16:7–11.

PARASITICAL

Consequently, they pay lip service to getting people saved, but devote little energy to that effort. Their brief, mechanical altar calls, if they give any at all, are little more than passing efforts. Their entire movement depends on someone else winning souls to God. Only then do they come on the scene to elevate these to new levels of knowledge. As such, their teaching must be viewed as parasitical.

In other words, if there were not true preachers of the gospel bringing people to Christ, the so-called modern faith teaching would ultimately disappear simply because they bring precious few to Christ themselves. In fact, it was the same identical way with the apostle Paul. The Judaizers who did not win any souls to Christ, and in fact could not win any souls to Christ, had to feed off of those whom Paul had won to the Lord. So the problem continues.

As a result, these so-called faith teachers have very little regard for world evangelism, at least as we think of such, except in limited settings. This is not surprising in that their teaching of higher knowledge does not readily appeal to people in many parts of the world.

They do, however, mention "thousands saved." This fits in with their confession concept. Even though there are few if any outward results, they tend to confess great results, pulling it out of thin air. In other words, there have been precious few salvations, if any.

They also imply that the believer no longer really needs God's grace, but is himself invested with the ability to do what is necessary in life. Hence, one hears a great deal about the ability of God in the believer. In other words, the believer becomes something of a free agent or a franchisee, doing all sorts of great things.

PRESUMPTION

When this is carried to its conclusion, it completely ignores the will of God, falling into the error of presumption and leaving the believer out of God's will, exercising instead his own judgment and will which is the ultimate sin. He will then commit Satan's sin of using God's Word against His (God's) purposes. Individuals are told to confess anything into existence—from Cadillacs to resurrection—completely ignoring the will of God in the matter. They say this is their right in their new knowledge in Christ Jesus.

As we have previously stated, they basically deny the sin nature, and teach that one cannot have a human nature and a godly nature at the same time. One is either totally divine or totally satanic, never just human.

We are told that man is either operating totally in the flesh realm (the world of the senses) or in the spiritual realm. Therefore, they would convince us that sickness is purely spiritual in origin and must be healed on that level alone instead of the physical level as well.

Consequently, they sometimes say that sickness is aligned with the sinful state of the ill person. It is always a spiritual problem (they say).

PHILOSOPHY

In view of all this, those adhering to this philosophy—and it is a philosophy; it is not the gospel—do not feel that Christians truly undergo trials or testings. If an individual appears to undergo such, then that person is operating, they say, in the realm of the senses, or in the flesh realm—the world of carnality or of Satan.

I don't know in what state they would have placed the apostle Paul, unless they claim, as some actually have, that if Paul had had their type of faith, he would not have had so many problems and difficulties.

They equate any individual living completely free from all difficulties or problems as operating in the world of the divine, which is God. It is always one or the other.

In their thinking, the individual is never just "human." Consequently, they would seldom say that they are tired or discouraged, etc. Converts are told never to confess any type of sickness. If they have a cold, they are to say (by faith) that they do not have a cold because confessing something of this nature would indicate humanity. As they tell it, they do not operate in the realm of the senses; they operate on a higher plane.

Anyone who prays, admitting total dependency on God, is filled with flaws and inconsistencies. To pray for God's help would be considered foolish by these people. They simply do not have flaws or inconsistencies. They have already arrived at a state of co-divinity with God.

PRIDE

These teachers seem blind to man's basic human nature and thereby appeal to man's pride. They do not seem to realize, or will not admit, that we are actually poor, undeserving creatures desperately in need of God's help, and due to the fall, we were born spiritually incomplete and inadequate, in need of a redeemer.

They do not seem to know or realize that only Jesus Christ is acceptable to God as our Savior and redeemer and that our relationship to God is according to our relationship with Christ, not some type of superior knowledge.

They also tend to forget that when we are saved (born again), our humanity does not cease. They ignore the fact that we still possess the flaws and inconsistencies of humans and thereby, continue to fall short of the glory of God, and only God's grace and mercy—through Jesus Christ and His Cross—allow us to enter into the presence of God. They lose sight of the fact that within ourselves we are unworthy and therefore totally dependent upon the Lord for His mercy and His grace.

AN IMPROPER KNOWLEDGE
OF THE CROSS OF CHRIST

This teaching, as stated, has an incomplete or faulty knowledge of the Cross of Jesus Christ. When one has a faulty knowledge of the Cross, basically their knowledge is faulty for the balance of the effort as well. They basically teach that Jesus Christ became a partaker of the satanic nature on the Cross. In other words, they suggest that He became identified with Satan. They claim He could not have died physically without first dying spiritually.

They seem to say, concerning the mortality of the body of Christ, that His death on the Cross was proof that He had ceased being the Son of God. They have a complete misconception of the incarnation of Christ as the perfect sacrifice—a sin offering.

Whether they realize it or not, they are teaching that Jesus was both divine and satanic, but not at the same time. In their view, He was divine while in His earthly ministry but became sinful while on the Cross as He took our sins upon Himself.

One must understand that it is not possible to be a sinner unless one sins. So they are somehow saying that Jesus sinned. They can't have it any other way.

The logical extension of their philosophy is that when Jesus took our sins upon Himself on the Cross, He became personally in need of redemption because of those sins. In short, because of this, they say that He died spiritually, went to hell (and we speak of the burning side of hell), as any sinner goes to hell upon the time of death, and, as a result, had to be born again exactly as we have to be born again.

They flaunt the Scripture which says He was the firstborn of many brethren, and they distort this to suggest that He was born again (in the sense of a spiritual birth). They seem to ignore the fact that Him being the firstborn of many brethren refers to Him as the author of the salvation plan (Rom. 8:29).

GNOSTICISM

Irenaeus, the ancient teacher who so strongly refuted Gnosticism (superior knowledge), which is so similar in many respects to the modern faith teaching, said "No creed is so blasphemous as theirs …, cutting off and dividing Jesus from Christ, Christ from Savior, Savior from Word, and Word from only begotten."

Modern faith teachers, which is actually not faith at all, at least that which God will recognize, claim that Jesus took on our satanic flesh on the Cross and then died. They use the scriptural reference of II Corinthians 5:21, completely pulling it out of context. They imply that the Cross is the place of the spiritual death of Jesus, in addition to His physical death.

In truth, this borders on blasphemy. It would seem that the power and forgiveness provided in the atonement of the Lord

Jesus Christ is lost to them, rejecting as they do their need for anything beyond knowledge.

One has the feeling that they come close to repudiating Calvary, consequently making light of such songs as "The Old Rugged Cross," etc. This type of song is looked at by them with disdain. They protest that they do not want to identify with the death of the Lord Jesus Christ, only His resurrection. One cannot help but conclude that they do not feel they have to go through repentance and the Cross. As stated, it is ignored and treated as "past miseries."

Whether they realize it or not, such teaching also denies their salvation.

The truth is, as the apostle Paul said in Galatians 6:14, *"But God forbid that I should glory, save in the Cross of our Lord Jesus Christ, by whom the world is crucified unto me, and I unto the world."*

Perhaps this error is merely scriptural ignorance; however, the fact that one is not aware of error does not make the error any less destructive.

A GREAT LURE

Tragically, this teaching, because of its promise of worldly riches, holds out an exciting lure and attracts many followers. It attracts many because most Christians, sad to say, do not have the firm foundation they should have in the Word of God. Consequently, they are easy prey for this type of teaching. As stated, it has a powerful attraction.

The promise of instant riches appeals to the selfishness and greed in most people's hearts—even Christians. However, the only one getting rich is the preacher or teacher.

Because this teaching is covered with Scripture, although twisted and taken out of context, it has the apparent blessing of the Word of God, or so many would think. With these twin appeals—money and self-gratification—it exerts great allure. Individuals are promised instant health and wealth, and this is a heady gospel.

Miracles and healings are spoken of constantly when, in reality, there are few if any miracles, and precious few healings, if any. Trusting followers are led to believe that God is continually speaking to these teachers. While it is certainly true that God definitely does speak to His people, still the regularity and instant communication claimed by these individuals places the teacher or preacher in some type of spiritual atmosphere far above the lowly crowd.

FAITH?

As such, stupendous statements and claims are made—statements and claims having no documentation in fact. By "faith," great numbers are announced as being saved. Miracles are tossed about as common occurrences, but with little basic substance or fact backing them up. Carelessness with facts becomes rampant—all under the guise of "faith." The followers, often knowing little of the Word of God, are lulled into deception by eagerly accepting what really does not exist.

It sounds so scriptural to the unknowing ear and eye. It sounds so plausible. It appears to be the dream of man, the answer to the cry of those desiring victory within their lives. There is some truth, as we stated earlier, in what they teach as there is some truth in all error.

This of course is what makes the error so much more difficult to recognize. Error surrounded by truth finds it easy to entrap the unwary in its reaches.

Jesus told us we must judge a tree by the fruit it bears (Mat. 12:33; Lk. 6:43). For a moment, let us look at the "fruit" of the "faith ministry."

FRUIT

First of all, as previously stated, very little priority is placed on winning souls to Christ. Principle emphasis is placed on money, healings, miracles, faith, knowledge, etc. Very little concern is demonstrated for the very core of true Christian faith—the salvation of the lost.

Second, the taking of the gospel of Jesus Christ to a lost world is little heeded. Consequently, areas of the world that cannot give a monetary return are, for the most, part ignored. This within itself is a complete denial of the Great Commission and actually denies the last words left by Christ before His ascension (Mk. 16:15–20).

And finally, this teaching will not lead to victory in the hearts and lives of any individuals because it is not scriptural. Any teaching that ignores the Cross, denies the Cross, or understates the Cross, is false. It is just that simple—it is false. In all cases, if followed to its conclusion, it will lead instead to future difficulties. People are promised all sorts of physical and material rewards, but very few of these promises ever materialize. Of course those who do not see these promises come to pass are labeled as not having enough faith.

Consequently, the believer is led to expect many things that God has never promised. Then when the expectant results fail to materialize, the individual ends up disappointed, at the least, and embittered at the worst.

IT JUST DOESN'T WORK

When real tragedy befalls, as it does in many lives, and this teaching of laws and formulas is applied, to the believer's dismay, it just doesn't work. The believers have been promised that these are God's laws, while in actuality they are nothing more than man's laws.

It is in this way that many, due to this teaching, have abandoned their walk with God and become embittered. They end up denying God, His work, His church, and everything that real salvation comprises—all because they believed with their hearts a premise built on a foundation of sand. The spiritual shores are littered with the wrecks of these hapless individuals. They placed their all in a false doctrine, but instead of gaining all, they lost all.

Sadly, these victims are ignored. There is no compassion for "faith drop-outs." They are dismissed with a flippant

"They missed it" and brushed aside like so much debris because there is always a fresh crop of gullible believers to take their place.

In closing, I must echo the words of Christ: *"Except a corn of wheat fall into the ground and die, it abides alone: But if it die, it brings forth much fruit. He who loves his life shall lose it; and he who hates his life in this world shall keep it unto life eternal. If any man serve Me, let him follow Me; and where I am, there shall also My servant be: If any man serve Me, him will My Father honor"* (Jn. 12:24–26).

Will you come, will you come, with your poor broken heart,
Burdened and sin oppressed?
Lay it down at the feet of your Savior and Lord.
Jesus will give you rest.

Will you come, will you come? There is mercy for you,
Balm for your aching breast;
Only come as you are, and believe on His name,
Jesus will give you rest.

Will you come, will you come? You have nothing to pay;
Jesus, who loves you best,
By His death on the Cross purchased life for your soul,
Jesus will give you rest.

Will you come, will you come? How He pleads with you now!
Fly to His loving breast;
And whatever your sin or your sorrow may be,
Jesus will give you rest.

How The Holy Spirit Works

CHAPTER 7

SALVATION

SALVATION

"FOR WE ARE SAVED by hope: But hope that is seen is not hope: For what a man sees, why does he yet hope for?" (Rom. 8:24).

FOR WE ARE SAVED BY HOPE

Until one understands the Cross of Christ, one does not properly understand the gospel of Christ. The Cross of Christ is the foundation of the gospel. In other words, everything is made possible by the Cross.

The heading refers to three things:

1. We have been saved, we are being saved, and we shall be saved. This statement has to do with several things, but primarily the fact that we must continue to trust and believe. Paul's statement completely refutes the unscriptural doctrine of unconditional eternal security, which teaches that once a person is truly saved, he cannot lose his salvation irrespective of what he may do or not do. In other words, the grace of God in this belief system is taken to the extreme.

2. As the Bible uses the word *hope,* it is a guarantee of something that is coming to pass in the future but is not known exactly when.

3. The word *hope* as used here tells us that the greater part of our salvation is yet future. We have now been sanctified, and we have been justified; however, we have not yet been glorified. That great event will take place at the coming resurrection when we will then realize the totality of what Jesus did in the atonement at Calvary's Cross (I Cor. 6:11).

BUT HOPE THAT IS SEEN IS NOT HOPE

The phrase proclaims in another way the great truth that all salvation affords is not yet given unto the believer. In fact, as far as the natural is concerned, we have not seen and neither can we see, at least at the present, that which is yet to come, except by faith.

This statement completely refutes the erroneous doctrine that claims Christianity is going to gradually take over the world by political means, and has already made great strides in this direction, with some even claiming that we are now living in the millennium.

False doctrines arise because of three things:

1. Ignorance of the Word of God
2. Knowledge of the Word, but unbelief regarding what it says
3. Misinterpreting the Word because of pride

If a person looks deep enough, he will find that all false doctrine begins with an improper understanding of the Cross, or a denial of the Cross, or unbelief as it regards the Cross. This means that all biblical doctrine is based squarely on the Cross of Christ. In fact, the Cross, at least as far as we know, was the first biblical doctrine, which was formulated in the mind of the Godhead from before the foundation of the world (I Pet. 1:18-20).

Let us say it again: The Cross of Christ is the foundation on which all Bible doctrine is based. If men base their doctrine on anything else, it will always be spurious.

FOR WHAT A MAN SEES, WHY DOES HE YET HOPE FOR?

In effect, the heading tells us bluntly that what is coming, as stated, is so far beyond that which is here at the present as to be no comparison. Hope is the absolute conviction and assured expectation. Such hope saves from oppression and animates the heart. It is the hope of verses 19 and 23.

BUT IF WE HOPE FOR THAT WE SEE NOT

"But if we hope for that we see not, then do we with patience wait for it" (Rom. 8:25).

The Cross of Christ and the Cross of Christ alone makes possible this hope. The Cross opened the door for everything that we receive from God, without which it would be impossible.

The heading tells us plainly all that salvation affords is not yet here. This speaks of the believer and the great change that is coming respecting the physical body.

It also speaks of the entirety of creation and how it will be changed back to that which it originally was when first created by God before the fall. In other words, a restoration of all things is soon to come.

So that means that the world is not going to be destroyed by a meteorite, too many cars emitting poisonous fumes, etc. Rather, it is going to be restored. Of course this will not happen until the second coming of the Lord Jesus Christ.

THEN DO WE WITH PATIENCE WAIT FOR IT

The phrase proclaims the certitude of its coming, because the Holy Spirit has promised that it would.

We do not see all that the gospel holds out to us, but it is the object of our Christian hope nevertheless. It is as true and sure as the love of God, which in Christ Jesus reconciled us to Himself and gave us the Spirit of adoption, and therefore, we wait for it in patience.

The idea of Paul's statement is that just as sure as what we presently have, just as sure is that which is to come. Therefore, this patience produces a joy in the heart of the believer, which is the opposite of that of the world.

In other words, we presently enjoy so much what we now have in Christ Jesus that it gives us a double joy in the anticipation of that which is yet to come.

LIKEWISE THE SPIRIT ALSO
HELPS OUR INFIRMITIES

"Likewise the Spirit also helps our infirmities: For we know not what we should pray for as we ought: But the Spirit itself (Himself) *makes intercession for us with groanings which cannot be uttered"* (Rom. 8:26).

That which we understand about the Cross was basically given to us by the apostle Paul. Respecting salvation, the Cross was typed throughout the entirety of the Old Testament system respecting the sacrificial offerings. However, as it regards sanctification, in other words, how we live for God on a daily basis, that great truth was as well given to the apostle Paul.

Most of all, the Holy Spirit, who is God, lives within our hearts and lives which was made possible by what Jesus did at Calvary, in other words, the Cross of Christ made and makes it all possible. This is at least one of the things that makes the new covenant of such greater magnitude than the old covenant. For one to realize that God is with him and actually in Him (Jn. 14:17) is, in a sense, beyond comprehension. The idea is that as far as the person is concerned, God is directing all of His attention and help to that one person. Of course, we know that God is omnipresent, therefore everywhere, but still His help for the believer is of such a personal nature, even as we are told here, that it is as if all of God's power and wisdom are reserved for the one believer.

That is in no way meant to promote selfishness in the heart of the believer, but rather the extent of personal direction given by the Lord.

Before the Cross, the Holy Spirit although with believers, could not come into their heart and life to abide. While He could come into the hearts and lives of some few such as Prophets, to enable them to carry out their mission, when that was finished He would leave.

Why?

The reason is the blood of bulls and goats could not (Heb. 10:4) take away sins, so that means the sin debt was still there, which of course greatly hindered the Holy Spirit. He cannot have anything to do with sin in any capacity.

As well, whenever a believer died before the Cross, his soul and spirit did not go to heaven, but rather down into paradise. Actually they were captives of Satan there. They were kept next door so to speak of the place called Hell, with it being separated from Abraham's bosom by a great gulf (Lk. 16:19-31).

Even the great faith worthies of the Old Testament were held captive by Satan. As stated, the Evil One could not hurt them, but still they were his captives. That's why Paul wrote concerning Jesus going into Paradise, *"He led captivity captive"* (Eph. 4:8).

As stated, they had been captives of Satan, but now they've become a captive of Jesus Christ, all because of what He did at the Cross.

WHAT DID HE DO AT THE CROSS?

First of all, He atoned for all sin—past, present, and future—at least for all who will believe. This satisfied the demands of the broken law, of which all men were guilty. In other words, by the giving of Himself as a perfect sacrifice on Calvary's Cross, He satisfied the demands of the broken law, and let us say it again, for those who believe.

As well, He broke the grip of sin that had fastened itself to every single individual, to where the believer could go free and not be bound by the powers of darkness.

As we see, the Cross changed everything. Now there is no more need for the sacrifice of lambs on altars. There is no more need for the table of shewbread, the golden lampstand, or the altar of incense. And there is no need whatsoever for the holy of holies—all of that was fulfilled in Christ and what He did at the Cross.

Since the Cross, the Holy Spirit comes into the heart of every believer at the moment of conversion. As well, when a believer dies, his soul and spirit instantly goes to be with the Lord Jesus Christ in the portals of glory. Once again, it is all because of the Cross.

HE HELPS US

In the Greek, the word *helps* is *sunantilambano,* and it means, "the action of a person coming to another's aid by taking hold over against that person, of the load he is carrying." The one coming to help does not take the entire load, but helps the other person in his endeavor.

It speaks of the Holy Spirit indwelling the saint and coming to the aid of the saint in his spiritual problems and difficulties. This type of help does not take over the believer's responsibility for his part, or give him an automatic deliverance without any effort on his part. This kind of help lends a helping hand, so to speak, and allows the believer to work out his problems and overcome his difficulties with the help of the Holy Spirit. In fact, the Holy Spirit does it this way in order that we might learn responsibility, trust, and see our faith grow. It's like a little child—a parent doesn't do everything for the child, but rather teaches him to do for himself. It's all to bring us to a state of maturity. If the Holy Spirit did everything for us, without us having to do anything ourselves, this would not be good for the saint, as should be obvious.

THE HOLY SPIRIT

In other words, the Holy Spirit will not promote the laziness of the believer by having food brought to him, but He will help him to go out and find a job. Even in that, He will seldom bring the job to the person, but will take the person to the job, at least if he gets out and tries.

A perfect example is that of Ruth the Moabitess. She had accepted the God of Israel and had come into His covenant. However, needing food for Naomi and herself, she went out to glean in the fields, which was the custom in Israel of that day concerning people who had fallen, for whatever reason, on hard times.

The Scripture says, *"And her hap was to light on a part of the field belonging unto Boaz"* (Ruth 2:3).

In other words, she went out looking for a place to glean, not really knowing where to go, but the Holy Spirit drew her to a certain place, even though she thought it just happened by chance. However, nothing is by chance concerning the child of God.

She didn't stay home, thereby telling the Holy Spirit to bring the grain to her, but went out searching for a way to find food. As stated, the Holy Spirit helped her, as He will help any who seeks to help themselves.

INFIRMITIES

In the Greek, the word *infirmities* is *astheneia,* and it means "want of strength, weakness."

The weakness spoken of here is defined by the context which speaks of prayer—one of the things in the spiritual realm in which our weakness needs His power. Although, the word *infirmities* could speak of physical needs, it basically speaks, at least here, of that which is spiritual.

The Holy Spirit through the apostle is telling us how He wants to help us, and how that it is done. We find it in the next phrase.

FOR WE KNOW NOT WHAT WE SHOULD PRAY FOR AS WE OUGHT

The heading proclaims prayer as the vehicle through which these things are carried out.

The weakness addressed here concerns the inability of the saint to know what to pray for. We do know what the general objects of prayer are, but we do not know what the specific, detailed objects of prayer in any given emergency or situation are.

In the Greek, the definite article is used before the word *what*. Consequently, Paul actually said we do not know "the what" we should pray for. In other words, the particular what.

In the Greek, the phrase *"As we ought"* is "katho dei," and it means, "What is necessary in the nature of the case for that we are to pray."

According as the need is at the moment, we know the end, which is common to all who pray, but we do not know what is necessary at each crisis of need to enable us to attain this end.

The subject of prayer is of such importance that it needs greater treatment than just a few lines.

BUT THE SPIRIT ITSELF

The heading should have been translated, "The Spirit Himself ..." and for specific reasons. The Holy Spirit is not an "it," but rather a person, and should have been addressed by the translators accordingly.

In the Greek, the word *intercession* as used here is, huperentunchano, and it means, "To make a petition or intercede on behalf of another, or on behalf of."

MAKES INTERCESSION FOR US

There are two major directions concerning the word *intercession* as it is used here:

1. This is intercession in respect to prayer, and not intercession on behalf of one who has sinned. This can only be
carried out by Christ, which He does constantly. The
Scripture says, *"Seeing He ever lives to make intercession
for them"* (Heb. 7:25). The Holy Spirit does not make
this type of intercession, only Christ. We will address
ourselves to the intercession of Christ when we get to
Romans 8:34.

2. The type of intercession made by the Holy Spirit on our
behalf in the realm of prayer is varied, even as we have
already studied. However, this intercession includes the
manner and way for approaching a king, in other words,
protocol. The Greek word is *enteuxis,* and is normally
the noun used for "prayer." However, inasmuch as Paul
uses verbs relative to intercession, it does not show up
in verses 26 or 27 of Romans 8.

Nevertheless, the Holy Spirit not only directs our attention
for what we should pray, but as well makes certain that what is
said before the
Father is terminology befitting a king, and in this case, the
Lord of glory.

A PERSONAL EXPERIENCE

As an example, I have had the occasion to meet the president of the United States on three separate occasions, as well as
other world leaders. Due to their offices, one observes certain
protocol, as would be obvious. In other words, a person doesn't

just barge in on the president as he might when visiting a friend. When meeting a person of such high office, there are certain things that one does, and certain things that one does not do.

Using that as an example, it would hold even truer for the Creator of all the ages. Consequently, the Holy Spirit makes certain that we approach God as we should, even though within ourselves we do not have such knowledge.

What a mighty God we serve!

WITH GROANINGS WHICH CANNOT BE UTTERED

The heading speaks of a burden of prayer that comes straight from the heart, and cannot really be put into words, at least successfully. This tells us that the Lord looks at the state of the heart that approaches the throne of God. In other words, the Holy Spirit is little interested in pious platitudes or beautiful phraseology in prayer. He is looking for a soul searching for God; one that cries to Him to such an extent that such a burden cannot really be put into words. Consequently, it can only be expressed in groanings.

In the Greek, the word *groanings* is *stenagmos,* and it means, literally, "a cry."

Many times in prayer the Holy Spirit will move through me in exactly this manner. The tears will begin to come as the Lord takes me into the very throne room of God. There is no way that one can properly express these times except with tears. At the same time, while the weeping or crying comes from my heart, it is actually the Holy Spirit who is moving upon me for this type of prayer to go forth. I personally feel it is the highest type of prayer.

This I do know: In times of prayer such as these, when the Holy Spirit does move in this fashion, in my own spirit, I feel that I have gotten through to the throne of God. To fully describe what has happened, one is unable. At the same time, there is a peace that fills one's heart at these times, because beyond a shadow of a doubt, that which the Holy Spirit wanted has been done.

ASKING AND RECEIVING FROM GOD

Considering how many promises we have in the Bible respecting prayer, and considering how Paul has brought it out extensively as to how the Holy Spirit helps us in this effort—especially how this type of intercession, which is the only type the Holy Spirit gives, is brought about only through prayer—then by all means we should take advantage of this tremendous privilege.

The very idea that a mere mortal has the opportunity and privilege of going before the God of all the ages, and is even encouraged to do so, and knowing that He can do all things, presents a privilege of unparalleled proportions. Yet most Christians take little advantage of this which is so very, very important.

Even though we have titled the beginning of this dissertation, "Asking and receiving from God," this only makes up a small part of prayer. Prayer is for consecration, dedication, and thanksgiving to the Lord for all that He has done for us, for the will of God to be realized in our lives, and for introspection by the Holy Spirit. In other words, there are really only three ways that one can properly communicate with the Lord:

1. The Word of God
2. Prayer
3. Worship

If the believer lets down on any one of these three, sad will be the results.

THE HOLY SPIRIT

In 1988, in the month of March, the Lord gave me a promise that has been (and still is) of astounding proportions.

In prayer one particular morning, the Lord said to me, "I'm going to show you some things about the Holy Spirit you do not presently know."

That was all He said.

What did He mean?

Of course the Holy Spirit is God. Consequently, there are untold numbers of things about Him that I do not know, which goes for all of humanity. Yet I knew that the Lord had said something to me that was special, to say the least. He only told me that He would show me something, but He did not say when. At any rate, I had a promise, but it was actually some nine years before the Lord brought that great promise to fruition. The answer would come in the great revelation of the Cross; however, I had no knowledge whatsoever of that in 1988.

Back in 1991, the Lord directed me to begin two prayer meetings a day, which we began immediately. To be frank, I followed that regimen for over 10 years. Presently, due to my schedule, I do not meet with others, but I still hold to these two prayer meetings each day. What the Lord ultimately did, I personally don't think would have been done had it not been for those daily prayer meetings, and, in fact, a continued strong prayer life, which I have always had.

THE REVELATION OF THE CROSS

During those years of these prayer meetings day and night, I really did not know that for which I was actually seeking the Lord. In other words, I wasn't praying for any specific thing because I actually did not know what I really needed. The Lord did say the following to me, which actually was all that was said as far as direction was concerned.

He said, "Do not seek Me so much for what I can do, but rather for who I am." That's exactly what I did, and little by little, the Lord began to reveal Himself to me in a more personal way than I had ever known previously.

Then it happened.

It was sometime in the spring of 1997. I had gone to the office early, which I always did to get ready for our morning program over SonLife Radio (we did not have network television at that particular time). I was studying the book of Romans. While I was studying, all of a sudden it happened. The Spirit of the Lord began to open up to me the meaning of the great sixth chapter of the book of Romans. This is the great chapter where Paul tells the believer how to live for God. He first of all takes the believer straight to the Cross (Rom. 6:3-5). In a few words, he tells us how the believer is baptized into the death of Christ, which takes place at conversion. He is then buried with Him by baptism into death and then raised with Him in newness of life. In other words, that is the foundation of our Christian experience, and our sanctification. As well, the believer must understand that when Paul uses the word *baptizes,* at least as he uses here, he is not speaking of water, but rather of being baptized into Christ. He is using the word *baptized* figuratively.

It's the same as when John the Baptist used the same term when he said: *"I indeed baptize you* (this is the word used literally) *with water unto repentance: But He who comes after me is mightier than I, whose shoes I am not worthy to bear: He shall baptize you* (here the word is used figuratively) *with the Holy Spirit, and with fire"* (Mat. 3:11).

The Holy Spirit then showed me (and did so through the writings of Kenneth Wuest, the Greek scholar) the meaning of the word *sin* as it is used in Paul's writings, especially in Romans 6. He explained from the original Greek text (the way that it was originally written) that in effect, it referred to the sin nature.

I will not go into detail here, but the moment I began to read those words, the Holy Spirit began to quicken my heart and mind in order that I might properly understand this all-important aspect of Christian living. Tragically, most Christians don't have the foggiest idea what the sin nature actually is.

THE SIN NATURE

The sin nature is a result of the fall that took place in the garden of Eden. Man fell from his position of total God-consciousness down to the far lower level of total self-consciousness. Sin, which is disobedience to the Word of God, characterizes the person's life. In other words, his very nature is toward sin. In fact, before any person comes to Christ, he is totally dominated by the sin nature, 24 hours a day, seven days a week, meaning that God constitutes everything he does as sin. He knows nothing else simply because he cannot know anything else. Everything such a person does, in some way, is toward sin—hence the sin nature. In other words, his very nature becomes that of spiritual failure.

Instantly, as this great truth began to dawn on me, I knew this was the answer to my great question—*why?* If the believer doesn't properly understand the sin nature and how it works, and above all how to have victory over the sin nature, and we speak of believers here, then in some way the sin nature is going to rule and reign in the heart and life of the believer. It doesn't matter how zealous that person is for the Lord, or how consecrated he is to the Lord. If he does not understand the sin nature, then in some way the sin nature is going to rule him, and he will be left extremely perplexed.

I DON'T UNDERSTAND...

That's why the great apostle Paul said: *"For that which I do I allow* (understand) *not: For what I would, that do I not; but what*

I hate, that do I" (Rom. 7:15). Please notice that I place the word *understand* in parentheses, which is the way the verse should have been translated, i.e., *"for that which I do I* understand *not."*

This was before the Lord gave to the great Apostle the understanding of the Cross. To be sure, when Paul wrote this seventh chapter of Romans, he very well understood the Cross. He is telling us that if we do not understand and follow the teaching given in Romans 6, then we are bound to repeat Romans 7, which refers to the sin nature ruling and reigning in one's life.

We can say without fear of contradiction that every single believer who has ever lived has struggled with the sin nature. The tragedy is, most Christians stay in the Romans 7 all of their lives, which means the sin nature is ruling them all of this time, despite the fact that they love the Lord.

The only victory over the sin nature is that the believer place his or her faith exclusively in Christ and what Christ has done for us at the Cross, and maintain it exclusively in Christ and the Cross. The Cross alone is the answer for sin, there is no other. Unfortunately, the church staggers from one fad to the other trying to address this terrible problem of sin, but all to no avail.

Let me say it again: It is the Cross alone which gives us victory over sin because it was there that Jesus atoned for all sin—past, present, and future—at least for all who will believe (Rom. 6:3-5; I Cor. 1:17-18, 23; 2:2; Gal. 6:14; Col. 2:10-15).

The believer must understand that the Holy Spirit works exclusively by and through the sacrifice of Christ. That's what gives Him the legal means to do all that He does (Rom. 8:2). The Holy Spirit does not demand much of us, but He does demand one thing, and on that He will not bend. He demands that our faith be exclusively in Christ and what Christ did for us at the Cross. That being done, He who is God, will work mightily on our behalf.

Going back to Paul, we find that He was trying with all of his zeal and strength to overcome, but he simply could not do so. That's why he said, "I don't understand what is happening." How many Christians at this moment are failing miserably, despite all they try to do otherwise (I speak of those who truly love the Lord, and who are struggling with all of their strength and might to be what they ought to be in the Lord. They will never find victory until they understand that this victory is in the Cross).

THE TRUTH

I found out later from my study of the Word that as the Lord first of all gave me the understanding of the sin nature, likewise, this is the way it was with Paul. Actually, the sin nature is approached by believers in one of several ways:

• *Ignorance (of the sin nature)*. Regrettably, even though it's one of the most important aspects of the believer's life, most Christians don't have the foggiest idea what the sin nature actually is. They are ignorant of what the Bible teaches in this respect. In the church I came up in, and it was a good church with a godly pastor, I'll admit that in all of those years, I didn't hear one single message on the sin nature. Also, I read hundreds and hundreds of books about the gospel, but I never read one single message about this all-important subject. This means that whoever was preaching in our pulpit, and whoever was writing the books did not know what the sin nature was. In fact, the modern church is still ignorant of this all-important truth.

• *License.* Some few have some knowledge of the sin nature but come to the conclusion that because they have a sin nature, sin is excused. In other words, they think, "Even though I am a Christian, I cannot help but to sin every day." The apostle Paul answered this by saying, *"Shall we continue in sin, that grace may abound?"* His answer was concise and to the point: *"God forbid."* (Rom. 6:1-2). Remember, the Lord saves us *from* sin, not *in* sin. Actually, the chief work of the Holy Spirit is to rid sin from our lives. While the Bible does not teach sinless perfection, it most definitely does teach that sin is not to have dominion over us (Rom. 6:14).

• *Denial.* Believe it or not, despite all the teaching in the Word of God concerning this subject, there are many who claim that once a person comes to Christ, the sin nature is gone—that is if they understand anything at all about the sin nature. In other words, they have no sin nature, or so they say. Now that's strange considering that Paul mentions the sin nature some 17 times in Romans 6 alone. Actually, there is one time that it does not really refer to the sin nature, but to acts of sin, which is in verse 15. In the original Greek language, which is the language of the New Testament, at least some 15 times in Romans 6 the word *sin* has what is referred to as the "definite article" in front of it. In other words, in the original language it actually reads: "*the* sin." This means that it is not actually speaking of acts of sin, but rather the evil nature, or the sin nature, with both meaning the same thing. That's the trouble with the church presently—it mostly treats the symptoms of sin, instead of what is causing the sin. So to deny that the believer has a sin nature, especially in the face of a mountain of evidence otherwise, is foolishness indeed. To be sure, the Holy Spirit would not have spent as much time as He did in explaining this subject for it not to exist.

• *Struggle.* There are many good Christians, and I speak of those who are truly consecrated to the Lord and struggle daily with the sin nature simply because they do not know or understand how it is to be addressed. In other words, they don't understand the sin nature and they don't understand the Cross. So, their Christian experience is one gigantic struggle, which to be frank is a far cry from the more abundant life spoken of by Christ (Jn. 10:10). In truth, there is a struggle with each and every believer, but it is with faith, which Paul referred to as a *"good fight"* because it is the right fight. That's the only fight we are called upon to engage, and that is the fight we are engaging, whether we realize it or not. Satan wants your faith in anything except the Cross of Christ, because it was at the Cross where he and all of his minions of darkness were defeated. Someone has said, and rightly so, that every attack by Satan, whether physical, financial, social, or spiritual, is for but one purpose and that is to destroy our faith, or at least to seriously weaken it.

• *Grace.* Of all the things we have listed—ignorance, license, denial, and struggle—grace is the only legitimate factor. This is the only way that the sin nature can be properly addressed. When the individual comes to Christ, the sin nature is made dormant. In other words, it should not cause anyone any problem whatsoever. However, if we attempt to live for God in the wrong way, which denies the grace of God, then we will find ourselves once again being ruled by the sin nature. If we keep our faith in Christ and the Cross and understand that it's the Cross that makes the power of the Holy Spirit available, then the grace of God can flow uninterrupted in our hearts and lives and give us perpetual victory, which means that the sin nature causes no problems. Regrettably, most Christians are frustrating the grace of God, which means they are trying to live for God with only a small part of the help that the Holy Spirit can give. In other words, He is greatly hindered when the sin nature rules a believer. In other words, He cannot do nearly what He is capable of doing because the sin nature is predominant. Regrettably, most Christians are frustrating the grace of God, which means they are trying to live for God with precious little help from the Holy Spirit. To be sure, the Holy Spirit will always do everything He can do, but He cannot function in our lives when we are ruled by the sin nature, meaning we are actually living in a state of spiritual adultery (Rom. 7:1-4; II Cor. 11:1-4). Paul said, *"I do not frustrate the Grace of God: for if righteousness come by the law, then Christ is dead in vain"* (Gal. 2:21). The grace of God works exclusively by and through the Cross of Christ. It only remains for our faith to be anchored in Christ and the Cross, which guarantees the grace of God. This means that we are doing it God's way. If we place our faith in anything else, no matter how good that anything else is, this means we frustrate the grace of God, which means that God cannot do for us what He wants to do. He has a way, and that way is the Cross; and if we place our faith therein, we get the help the Holy Spirit can give, which is the key to all victory (Rom. 6:1-14; 8:1-11; I Cor. 1:17-18, 23; 2:2; Gal. 6:14; Col. 2:10-15).

THE CROSS OF CHRIST

The following is what the Lord gave to me in 1997 as the solution for the sin nature:

- "The answer for which you seek is found in the Cross of Christ."
- "The solution for which you seek is found in the Cross of Christ."
- "The answer for which you seek is found only in the Cross of Christ."

I was now beginning to understand the scriptural rudiments of sanctification. As wave after wave of the Spirit of God swept over my soul that morning in 1997, I knew that what the Lord was giving to me was greater than I could even begin to comprehend. I remember requesting of Him that this door never close, but that I keep learning. Knowing that I could not exhaust the potential of the Cross—the finished work of Christ—I asked the Lord if He would continue to open that door to me.

In other words, I wanted Him to give me more and more under-standing of this great truth, i.e., the atonement.

THE OBJECT OF MY FAITH

There is very seldom a day that I do not learn a little more about the finished work of Christ. It is a perfect work. It is so perfect that it will never have to be amended. This is the reason Paul called it *"the everlasting covenant"* (Heb. 13:20).

From the information given by the Holy Spirit to me as it regards the Cross, I knew that the Cross must be the object of my faith. Incidentally, when the Lord gave me this, He once again took me to the great sixth chapter of Romans.

From the information given by the Holy Spirit to me as it regards the Cross, I knew that the Cross must be the object of my faith. To be sure, that is so very, very important. The major problem with most Christians is an improper object of faith. In other words, they are placing their faith in something that may be good in its own right, but it's the wrong place for their faith. Our faith must be exclusively in Christ as the source of all things, and the Cross as the means of all of these things given to us.

After the Lord gave me this truth regarding the Cross, which was not new but that which had been given to the apostle Paul long ago, the thoughts entered my mind as to how the Holy Spirit figured into all of this. I knew that He did, but I didn't understand how.

For several weeks I cried to the Lord about this thing, asking Him to show me. Then it happened.

THE HOLY SPIRIT

The following has been given in this volume, but due to its significance, please allow the repetition.

It happened one morning a few weeks after the Lord had given me the revelation of the Cross. Actually, we were in the midst of our radio program, *A Study in the Word* which aired five days a week. Loren Larson was on the program with me. The program which lasted an hour and thirty minutes was almost over. Then the Holy Spirit spoke through me in a way that I had never previously experienced.

Without premeditation, I made the statement, "The Holy Spirit works entirely within the framework of the finished work of Christ." I went on to say, *"He will not work outside of that framework, which demands that we have faith exclusively in Christ and what Christ did for us at the Cross."*

It somewhat shocked me when these words came out of my mouth, because they were not premeditated. Actually, I had never heard the statement before in my life, and I had never read such in a book. All I could do after I made the statement was to sit there in silence pondering where it came from. Then Loren spoke up and said, "Can you give me Scripture for that?"

I sat there for a few more moments wondering how I could give Scripture when it was something I had not thought of, studied, or previously known. For the few short moments I was sitting there, silent, I began to realize how momentous, how stupendous, and how glorious the statement I had just made was. Then I looked down at my Bible, and it was open to Romans 8. The Holy Spirit quickly pointed out verse 2, and I read it out loud: *"For the law of the spirit of life in Christ Jesus has made me free from the law of sin and death."* When I said it, the Spirit of the Lord entered the room. In a few moments, the program ended. I stood up to leave the studio when all of a sudden the Lord moved on me again.

He said to me, *"Do you remember the promise I made to you back in 1988, how I would show you things about the Holy Spirit you did not then know?"*

Of course I did.

He then said, *"I have just kept My promise to you."*

In essence, the Lord told me that day how the Holy Spirit works within our lives as believers, which is an astounding truth.

HOW THE HOLY SPIRIT WORKS

First of all, and as previously stated, the Lord told me that the Holy Spirit works entirely within the framework of the finished work of Christ. In other words, what Jesus did at the Cross gave—and gives—the Holy Spirit the legal right to do all that He does in our hearts and lives—that which He could not do before the Cross (Jn. 14:17).

For Him to work as He so desires, He only requires that our faith ever be in Christ and the Cross. Then He will do great things within our lives, bringing about righteousness and holiness (Rom. 6:3-5, 11, 14; 8:1-11).

As believers, we are married to Christ (Rom. 7:1-4; II Cor. 11:1-4). Being married to Christ, He is to meet our every need, and in fact is the only one who can meet our every need. We are to look to Him exclusively, and we do so by exhibiting faith in Him and the work that He did for us at the Cross.

LOOKING TO CHRIST AND THE CROSS

If we look elsewhere we are, in essence, committing spiritual adultery, which as one would automatically know, greatly hinders the Holy Spirit. Thank God that He doesn't leave us, but He can do very little for us while we are in a state of spiritual adultery, and I speak of having victory over sin. That is so important that I need to say it again: If we place our faith in anything, no matter how good that other thing might be, and it's not Christ and the Cross, then the Lord constitutes it as spiritual adultery.

I'll say it again: We are being unfaithful to Christ. This greatly hinders the Spirit of God and grieves Him to a great extent.

We are to place our faith exclusively in Christ and what Christ did for us at the Cross, which will then guarantee the work of the Holy Spirit. Understanding that He is God, this means that He will do anything and everything for us that is needed. That's how the Holy Spirit works, which I believe is one of the greatest revelations given by the Holy Spirit at this particular time. When I say "revelation" I'm not meaning something new, for it isn't. It is that which was given originally to the apostle Paul, and Paul gave it to us in his 14 epistles.

As we have already stated in this volume, before the Cross, the Holy Spirit was greatly limited as to what He could do because the blood of bulls and goats could not take away sins (Heb. 10:4).

For instance, He could not come into the hearts and lives of all believers, only a select few such as prophets, and when the work was finished, He would leave. Now of course, since the Cross, the moment a person comes to Christ—at that moment—the Holy Spirit comes into his heart and life and is there to abide forever (Jn. 14:16-18).

As well, before the Cross, when a believer died, his soul and spirit did not go to heaven, but rather down into paradise, where he was actually a captive of Satan. In other words, his being liberated from that place and taken to glory depended totally on the Cross of Christ. Thank God that ultimately the Cross became a reality, and then Satan had no more claim on those believers. What the blood of bulls and goats could not do, the shed blood of Christ was most able to carry out.

Regrettably, if a person were to ask Christians about how the Holy Spirit works, most would look at him with a blank stare. In fact, most Christians think that the work of the Holy Spirit is something that is automatic, in other words, it just happens. Nothing could be further from the truth.

Let us say it again: The Holy Spirit does not require much of us, but He does require one thing, and on that He will not bend. He requires that our faith be exclusively in Christ and what Christ has done for us at the Cross, and that our faith be maintained exclusively in Christ and what He has done for us at the Cross. That being done, the Holy Spirit will work mightily within our hearts and lives.

We must understand that what is impossible for us is not impossible for Him at all, considering that He is all-powerful, and considering that He is God. That's how the Holy Spirit works.

———⸺◇⸺———

Souls of men, why will you scatter
Like a crowd of frightened sheep?
Foolish hearts, why will you wander
From a love so true and deep?

Was there ever kindest shepherd
Half so gentle, half so sweet,
As the Saviour who would have us
Come and gather round His feet?

There's a wideness in God's mercy
Like the wideness of the sea,
There's a kindness in His justice
Which is more than liberty.

There is welcome for the sinner,
And more graces for the good;
There is mercy with the Saviour
There is healing in His blood.

There is plentiful redemption
In the blood that has been shed;
There is joy for all the members
In the sorrows of the Head.

For the love of God is broader
Than the measures of man's mind;
And the heart of the Eternal
Is most wonderfully kind.

But we make His love too narrow
By false limits of our own;
And we magnify its strictness,
With a zeal He will not own.

If our love were but more simple
We should take Him at His Word:
And our lives would be all sunshine
In the sweetness of our Lord.

HOW THE HOLY SPIRIT WORKS

THE MIND OF
THE SPIRIT

THE MIND OF THE SPIRIT

"AND HE WHO SEARCHES the hearts knows what is the mind of the Spirit, because He makes intercession for the saints according to the will of God" (Rom. 8:27).

AND HE WHO SEARCHES THE HEARTS

The heading speaks of God the Father. Actually all three persons of the Trinity search the heart:

- God the Father (I Chron. 28:9; Jer. 17:10)
- the Son (Rev. 2:23)
- and the Spirit (I Cor. 2:10)

However, there is a progression of order here that is not to be ignored. Even though the Holy Spirit is God and consequently knows all things, still, His purpose and agenda is to carry out the will of God in our lives, even as the last phrase in this verse proclaims.

One could say that the Father orchestrates, the Son institutes, and the Spirit executes.

KNOWS WHAT IS THE MIND OF THE SPIRIT

The heading refers to the special means of communication, which can refer to praying in tongues, but not necessarily so.

The idea is that God the Father, who searches the hearts of His saints, understands the intent or bent of our unutterable prayers. They are unutterable because we do not know the particular things for which we should pray in connection with a certain circumstance. God the Father knows the mind of the Holy Spirit praying for us—and in our stead—according to the plan of God for our lives.

Even though the text is speaking of the personal work of the Holy Spirit on behalf of the saints, on a general basis at this particular time (2018), that which the Holy Spirit is presently saying to the churches, I personally believe is the Message of the Cross.

In other words, the church should come back to the Cross. I say come back, but in reality most of the church had never been there to begin with.

BECAUSE HE MAKES INTERCESSION FOR THE SAINTS ACCORDING TO THE WILL OF GOD

The heading refers to the fact that the Holy Spirit is ensconced within our hearts and lives to carry out God's will and not our will. He is not there to do our bidding, but the bidding of the Father, simply because the Father knows what we need.

The idea of all of this is twofold:

1. *The will of God.* For the will of God to be carried out in the life of the believer, there must be a strong prayer life involved. As well, our faith must be anchored exclusively in Christ and what He has done for us at the Cross. The will of God always begins at the Cross, and for us to have that will and to know that will, we must first of all understand the Cross of Christ respecting not only salvation, but also our sanctification.

2. *The plan of God.* God has a plan for the entirety of the world, as well as a plan for each believer. This plan is ever the priority of the Spirit respecting our hearts and lives. He has the overall plan in mind as well as our personal involvement in that plan. He is there for one purpose: realizing this that God desires. As we have stated, this plan can only be worked out as we understand that it is the Cross of Christ that makes everything possible. In other words, for every single thing that the Lord gives us, it is the Cross of Christ that opened that door. For the believer to work at odds with that which the Lord desires—and I speak of having faith in something other than Christ and the Cross—only creates conflict.

THE CROSS OF CHRIST

Paul said, *"Because the carnal mind is enmity against God: For it is not subject to the law of God, neither indeed can be"* (Rom. 8:7).

In the Greek, the word *enmity* is *echthra,* and it means "hostility, opposition, hatred."

The *"carnal mind"* speaks of anything other than faith in the Cross of Christ. This places such an individual in a very precarious situation. To be at odds with a fellow human being is one thing, but to be at odds with God is something else altogether.

The believer must understand the following: Man is in a dilemma in which he cannot extricate himself. In other words, he has no solution. God has all the solution and all the means and ways. It is all made possible by the Cross. When man seeks to find another way, even as Cain did so long ago, this angers God. It puts the person at odds with the Lord. It creates hostility.

So, let us say it again: One cannot know the plan of God for one's life until one's faith is anchored exclusively in Christ and what Christ did for us at the Cross. Anything else frustrates the grace of God, and thereby shuts the door to all that the Holy Spirit desires to do for us.

The patriarch, Jacob, is a perfect example. When his life was changed, it was the result of a wrestling match with God, which in effect was caused by self-will (Gen. Chpt. 32). In fact, self-will is the major problem in the lives of all believers. Someone has said, and rightly so, that when Jesus died on Calvary, He died there to save us not only from sin, but also from self.

THE MINISTRY OF INTERCESSION

Even though Romans 8:26-27 speaks primarily of intercession made by the Holy Spirit on our behalf, still incorporated in the text is the intercession that the Holy Spirit promotes in the hearts of praying believers as they intercede for others.

Actually, it is in this manner alone that various moves of God take place all over the world. This is the reason for revival in certain areas, for movings and operations of the Holy Spirit in certain parts of the world, and even for conviction respecting individuals. None of that just happens—it is carried out through the ministry of intercession on the part of believers. Of course, as stated, the Holy Spirit is the one who executes all of this.

To be a little clearer, the point I am attempting to make is that every single person in the world who is saved and every move of God that takes place somewhere (anywhere) has been brought about by intercession on the part of believers in some way. Believers doing the interceding may have been very much acquainted with the people or situation, or not acquainted with them at all. Even so, the Holy Spirit would begin to move upon the believer's heart respecting intercession for certain people, certain areas, or certain parts of the world. Many times these are areas where the intercessor has never been. At the same time, the Holy Spirit is probably moving on a number of intercessors all over the world respecting this particular area or place, with none of these people acquainted with each other, and yet the Holy Spirit is acquainted with all.

THE AUTHORITY OF THE BELIEVER

Even though the Lord needs nothing, He has allowed believers a very prominent part in the carrying out of His great plan on this earth. Actually, the involvement of believers in that plan is of such magnitude that if we fall down at our task, the work of God is very greatly hindered. Even though God's plan is ultimately realized—albeit sometimes delayed—what the believer does still affects that plan greatly, whether in a positive or negative sense.

The believer's great part in this is characterized as the Great Commission (Mat. 28:18-20; Mk. 16:15-20; Lk. 24:49; Acts 1:8).

Incidentally, as an aside, every believer in the world has spiritual authority. Of course, some have more than others; however, this spiritual authority is never over other people, but always over Satan and spirits of darkness—be they demons or fallen angels, etc.

Unfortunately, some have tried to claim spiritual authority for individuals, and as such, they should be obeyed no matter what they say. Nothing could be further from the truth. While we are to love every single believer in the world, our allegiance belongs to the Lord and none other.

Paul said regarding this very thing, and I quote from The Expositor's Study Bible: "*Owe no man anything* (carries the idea that Christians do not owe their brethren in the Lord the same obedience that is owed civil rulers [Rom. 13:1-7]), *but to love one another* (proclaims the only requirement between believers): *For he who loves another has fulfilled the law* (pertains to what the law of Moses intended, but wasn't able to bring about; it can be done under Christ, and Christ alone)" (Rom. 13:8).

INTERCESSION

In the Hebrew, *intercession* is *pagha,* and it means "to make intercession, to strike upon, or against, to assail anyone with petitions, to urge, and when on behalf of another, to intercede" (Gen. 23:8; Ruth 1:16; Job 21:15; Isa. 53:12; Jer. 7:16; 27:18; 36:25).

In the New Testament, a similar word is used in the Greek— *enteuxis*— among several other Greek words that mean "to come between, to interpose on behalf of, to intercede" (Rom. 8:26–34; I Tim. 2:1; 4:5). Actually, the Greek word *entugchano* is found in Romans 8.

MAN'S INTERCESSION FOR HIS FELLOWMAN

Many such prayers are recorded in Scripture:
- The sacrificial act of Noah may have been partly of this nature, for it is followed by a promise of God on behalf of the race and the earth at large (Gen. 8:20–22).
- Abraham's prayer for Ishmael (Gen. 17:18).
- Abraham's prayer for Sodom (Gen. 18:23–33).
- Abraham for Abimelech (Gen. 20:17).
- Jacob's blessing of Joseph's sons is also of the nature of intercession (Gen. 48:8–22). His dying blessing of his sons is hardly to be regarded as intercessory; it is rather declarative, although in the case of Joseph, it does approach intercession.

The absence of distinct intercessory prayer from Abraham to Moses is to be observed and shows, at least in part, the spiritual apathy of the time. In Moses, however, the social element finds a further development, and is interesting as taking up the Spirit of the Father of the faithful, namely Abraham.

The intercessory ministry of Moses is revealed in his prayer for the removal of the plagues regarding Egypt (Ex. 15:25); for water at Rephidim (Ex. 17:4); for victory over Amalek (Ex. 17:8–16); and prayer for the people after the golden calf (Ex. 32:11–14, 21–34; 33:12). There are many other instances as well.

MOSES

None of these prayers of Moses' are perfunctory. They are the vivid and passionate utterances of a man full of divine enthusiasm and love for his people. It is intercession wrung from a great and devout soul on occasions of deep and critical importance.

In the history of Joshua, we find only the prayer for the people after the sin of Achan (Josh. 7:6–9), although the communications from God to Joshua are numerous. A faint intercessory note may be heard in Deborah's song as well (Judg. 5:13). Gideon's prayer seemed to reecho something of the words of Moses (Judg. 6:13). Manoah's prayers may be noted also (Judg. Chpt. 13).

However, for the most part, from Moses to Samuel, even as it had been from Abraham to Moses, there seems to have been very little intercession. Again, this shows the spiritual climate of that period.

THE KINGS AND THE PROPHETS

Samuel is the real successor of Moses, and in connection with his life, intercession again appears more distinct and effective. His mother Hannah's song, for instance, though chiefly of thankfulness, is not without the intercessory spirit (I Sam. 2:1–11). There is also Samuel's prayer at Mizpeh (I Sam. 7:5) and the recognition by the people of Samuel's place (I Sam. 7:8).

Going to others, one must note David's prayer for deliverance of the people from pestilence (II Sam. 24:17); Solomon's prayer for wisdom to govern the people (I Ki. 3:5–15); Solomon's prayer at the dedication of the temple (I Ki. 8:12–61); Elijah's prayer for the widow's son (I Ki. 17:20); Elijah's prayer for rain (I Ki. 18:42); Elisha's prayer for the widow's son (II Ki. 4:33); and Hezekiah's prayer (II Ki. 19:14–19).

Of course, there are many more of which we do not have space to enumerate.

Also, the poetic books furnish a few examples of intercessory prayer: Job's intercession for his children (Job 1:5); and the Lord's command that Job should pray for his friends even though they had not been very kind to him (Job 42:8).

In the prophetic books, the note of intercession also appears. The prophet, though primarily a messenger from God to man, has also something of the character of the intercessor (Isa. Chpt. 6). In Jeremiah 42:4, the prophet consents to the request of Johanan to seek the Lord on behalf of the people. The book of Lamentations is naturally conceived in a more constantly recurring spirit of intercession. In the prophecies, Jeremiah has been the messenger of God to the people. However, after the catastrophe, in his sorrow, he appeals to God for mercy upon them (Lam. 2:20; 5:1–19).

Ezekiel in the same way is rather the seer of visions and the prophetic representative of God. Yet at times he appeals to God for the people (Ezek. 9:8; 11:13).

INTERCESSION IN THE NEW TESTAMENT

In the New Testament, all prayer necessarily takes a new form from its relation to our Lord, and in these supplications before God, intercessory prayer plays its part.

At the outset, Jesus teaches prayer on behalf of those *"which despitefully use you"* (Mat. 5:44). How completely does this change the entire spirit of prayer! We breathe a new atmosphere of the high revelation of love as characterized by Christ. As well, the Lord's Prayer (Mat. 6:9–13) is of this character. In fact, Christ's high-priestly prayer is the most sublime height of prayer to God and is intercessory throughout (Jn. Chpt. 17).

THE ENTRANCE OF THE HOLY SPIRIT

Although the Holy Spirit has always been involved in man's prayer and petition to the heavenly Father and as well, in intercession, His filling the hearts of believers after the day of Pentecost due to what Jesus did at Calvary puts a brand-new perspective on this tremendous ministry.

It is even as we are now studying in Romans 8:26–27. While it seems as if the entirety of the text is devoted to the Spirit Himself interceding on behalf of believers, still, the word *helps* and the phrase, *"For we know not what we should pray for as we ought"* (v. 26), lets us know that He is actually the one who energizes the believer respecting intercession on behalf of others. Actually, the divine Spirit is said to be a Spirit of supplication (Zech. 12:10).

We see this intercession at work throughout the entirety of the book of Acts. Hence, the prayers of the early church believers become intercession at times, involving the wider outlook on others and on the world at large, which Christianity has bestowed on men. Actually, they literally breathe the Spirit (Acts 2:24–30; 6:6; 7:60; 8:24; 9:40; 12:5–12; 13:3; 14:23; 15:40; 20:36).

THE INTERCESSION OF CHRIST

Even though this ministry of Christ is on a far higher plane than that of believers, still the example is very prominent before all.

The general conception of our Lord's mediatorial office is especially summed up in His intercession in which He appears in His high-priestly office, and also as interceding with the Father on behalf of that humanity whose cause He has espoused.

The function of a priesthood, which was meant to emulate Christ, as developed under Judaism involved the position of mediation between man and God. The priest represented man, and on man's behalf approached God; thus, he offered sacrifice, interceded, and gave to the offerer whom he represented the benediction and expression of the divine acceptance.

In other words, forgiveness by the Lord was tendered toward the sinning soul.

HOW CHRIST INTERCEDES ON OUR BEHALF

Paul wrote:

But this man (the Lord Jesus Christ), *because He continues ever* (proclaims the priesthood of Christ as eternal, while death was inevitable as it regarded the Aaronic priests), *has an unchangeable priesthood.* (This not only refers to that which is eternal, but to that which will not change as far as its principle is concerned as well. The reason is the finished work of the Cross is an *'everlasting Covenant')"* (Heb. 13:20). *Wherefore He* (the Lord Jesus Christ) *is able also to save them to the uttermost* (proclaims the fact that Christ alone has made the only true atonement for sin; He did this at the Cross) *who come unto God by Him* (proclaims the only manner in which man can come to God), *seeing He ever lives to make intercession for them"* (His very presence by the right hand of the Father guarantees such, with nothing else having to be done [Heb. 1:3] (Heb. 7:24-25, The Expositor's Study Bible).

THE SACRIFICE OF CHRIST

The sacrifice of Christ has been accepted, and the very presence of Christ at the throne of God proves this. As well, His intercession on our behalf does not refer to certain particulars carried out by Himself, for the work has already been done. In other words, His very presence at the throne of God guarantees all on our behalf that is needed. We must remember that Calvary was a finished work.

If a person wants to know what the intercessory work of Christ is, he only has to look at the prayer of David—the prayer of repentance listed in the Psalm 51. In this prayer, our Lord becomes as us, thereby interceding on our behalf. Actually, the prayer is threefold:

1. As is obvious, it is David's prayer of repentance as it regards his terrible sin of adultery with Bath-Sheba and the murder of her husband, Uriah.

2. The prayer also characterizes Israel when she will cry to God—a cry of repentance during the battle of Armageddon, which will precipitate the second coming of the Lord Jesus Christ. In other words, this will also be Israel's cry and prayer of repentance.

3. Above all, this prayer pictures and portrays the intercessory prayer of Christ—all on our behalf. It has already been prayed, and our looking to Him guarantees the answer to that prayer.

THE WORK OF CHRIST

As in sacrifice, so in the work of Christ, we find the proprietary rights of the offerer in the sacrifice. For man, Christ as one with man, and yet in His own personal right, offers Himself (Rom. Chpt. 5; Gal. 4:5; Heb. 2:11).

There was also the transfer of guilt and its conditions, typically by laying hands on the head of the animal called the scapegoat, which then bore the sins of the offerer and was presented to God by the priest.

The acknowledgment of sin and the surrender to God is completely fulfilled in Christ's offering of Himself at His death (Lev. 3:2, 8, 13; 16:21; Isa. 53:6; II Cor. 5:21).

Our Lord's intercessory quality in the sacrifice of Himself is not only indicated by the imputation of guilt to Him as representing the sinner, but also in the victory of His life over death, which is then given to man in God's acceptance of Christ's representation and the substitution of Himself.

ITS INTERCESSORY CHARACTER

In the epistle to the Hebrews, the intercessory character of our Lord's high-priestly office is transferred to the heavenly condition and work of Christ, where the relation of Christ's work to man's condition is regarded as being still continued in the heavenly place (Heb. 9:11–28). This entrance into heaven is once for all, and in the person of the high priest, the way is open to the very presence of God.

From one point of view (Heb. 10:12) the priestly service of the Lord was concluded and gathered up into His kingly office (Heb. 10:13–18). From another point of view, we, in a sense, are bidden to enter into the holiest place, as if in union with Christ, we, too, become a kingly priesthood (Heb. 10:19–22; I Pet. 2:9).

THE RIGHT OF ENTRANCE

It must not be forgotten, however, that this right of entrance into the most holy place—the very throne of God—is one that depends entirely upon our vital union with Christ. He appears in heaven for us and us with Him, and in this sense He fulfills the second duty of His high-priestly office as intercessor, with the added conception drawn from the legal advocacy of the Roman court. We must understand that this right and privilege of going into the very throne of God—which actually belongs to every believer—is made possible totally and completely by Christ and what He did for us at the Cross. Once again, it's the Cross that opens the door to everything, even the very throne of God.

The term "Advocate" in I John 2:2 is, in the Greek, *parakletos,* which in John 14:16 is translated "Comforter." The word has a familiar use in Greek for the legal advocate in Roman law who appeared on behalf of his client. Thus, in the double sense of priestly and legal representation, our Lord is our intercessor in heaven. In other words, He guarantees our salvation and redemption, which is all made possible by the Cross. His legal representation is guaranteed by the seal of promise given by the Holy Spirit.

Concerning this Paul said:

And that He (Christ) *might reconcile both* (Jews and Gentiles) *unto God in one body* (the Church) *by the Cross* (it is by the atonement only that men ever become reconciled to God), *having slain the enmity thereby* (removed the barrier between God and sinful man): *And came and preached peace to you which were afar off* (proclaims the gospel going to the Gentiles) *and to them who were nigh* (this refers to the Jews. It is the same message however for both—Jews and Gentiles.) *For through Him* (through Christ) *we both* (Jews and Gentiles) *have access by One Spirit unto the Father"* (if the sinner comes by the Cross, the Holy Spirit opens the door, otherwise it is barred [Jn. 10:1]). (Eph. 2:16-18, The Expositor's Study Bible).

THE MANNER OF HIS REPRESENTATION

Of the modes in which Christ carries out His intercessory office, we can have little knowledge except so far as we may fairly deduce them from the phraseology and suggested ideas of Scripture. As high priest, it may surely be right for us to aid our weak faith by assuring ourselves that our Lord pleads for us, and does so by His very appearance at the throne of God, without actually having to say anything. At the same time, we must be careful not to deprave our thought concerning the glorified Lord by the metaphors and analogies of earthly relationship.

To be sure, His intercession on our behalf is done on a much higher plane and level than we can too very well comprehend.

Consequently, the intercessory work of Christ may be represented in these ways: He represents man before God in His perfect nature, His exalted office, and His completed work. The Scripture for this is *"To appear in the presence* (before the face)

of God for us" (Heb. 9:24). This plainly proclaims an active intercession. This is the office of our Lord as advocate or parakletos.
This conveys some relation to the aid one who has broken
the law receives from an advocate, and that cannot be overlooked. We find Christ's intercession in this aspect brought into
connection with the text, which referred to justification and its
allied ideas (Rom. 8:34; I Jn. 2:1).

THE MANNER OF INTERCESSION
AND REPRESENTATION

Whatever else it may include, the following must be a part
of that which the Lord does for us as our personal representative in heaven:

- His appearing before God on our behalf, as the sacrifice
  for our sins, as our High Priest on the ground of whose
  work we receive the remission of our sins, the gift of
  the Holy Spirit.
- Defense against the sentence of the law and the charges
  of Satan, who is the great accuser.
- His offering Himself as our surety, not only that the
  demands of justice shall be shown to be satisfied, but
  that His people shall be obedient and faithful.
- The oblation of the persons of the redeemed, sanctifying
  their prayers and all their services, and rendering them
  acceptable to God through the savor of His own merits.

Even this expression of the elements that constitute the
intercession of the Lord on our behalf, cautious and spiritual

as it is in its application to Christian thought and worship, must be carefully guarded from a too complete and materialistic use.

Without this care, worship and devout thought may be degraded and fall into the mechanical forms by which our Lord's position of intercessor has been reduced to very little more than an imaginative and spectacular process that goes on in some heavenly place.

It must not be forgotten that the metaphorical and symbolic origin of the ideas which constitute Christ's intercession (for instance, the duties of the high priests of old) is always in danger of dominating and materializing the spiritual reality of His intercessional office.

Nevertheless, even though of necessity our understanding is limited, the example portrayed by Christ in His intercessory role on our behalf should at least produce in us a love for the lost and especially for our fellow believers. While we may not understand all that He has done, is doing, and shall do, we still know that His intercession on our behalf is total and complete. Of that we can be certain.

(The author is indebted to L.D. Bevans for excerpts from his insights on the intercession of Christ.)

'Tis God the Spirit leads
In paths before unknown;
The work to be performed is ours,
The strength is all His own.

Supported by His grace,
We still pursue our way,
And hope at last to reach the prize,
Secure in endless day.

'Tis He who works to will
'Tis He who works to do,
This is the power by which to act,
This is the glory too.

How The Holy Spirit Works

CHAPTER 9

THE CALLED

THE CALLED

"AND WE KNOW THAT all things work together for good to them who love God, to them who are the called according to His purpose" (Rom. 8:28).

AND WE KNOW THAT ALL THINGS WORK TOGETHER FOR GOOD

As we have said before, let us say it again: Until one understands the Cross in both its salvation and sanctifying roles, one does not really understand the gospel. It is the Cross of Christ that makes everything possible. There are two key words in verse 28: love and purpose.

The heading presents the beginning of one of the most often quoted Scriptures in the Bible.

In view of the broad brush of this text, and especially considering its vast consequences, one would not do violence to Scripture by asking this question: Do, in fact, all things work together for good concerning believers?

The answer is yes and no. If the conditions are met, then yes. If the conditions are not met, then no.

Paul begins this great promise by saying *"We know,"* which means that not only does he know this, but as well it is meant for every other believer to know, hence the repetition of the text.

Also, *"all things"* covers the entirety of the spectrum respecting life and godliness (II Pet. 1:2-4). It refers to every effort made by Satan against the child of God, every scurrilous plan devised by him for our destruction, and even pertains to evil men working with him (whether they realize it or not) to further the designs of darkness concerning our own personal lives.

TO THEM WHO LOVE GOD

The heading proclaims the first qualification. However, in the Greek text, the apostle designates the believers as not merely loving God, but being beloved by God. The divine side of our security from harm is brought out, as combining with and insuring the other. We are sure that all things work for our good, not only because we love Him who works all things, but also because He who works all things has loved and chosen us and carried us through the successive steps of our spiritual life.

So we learn from this passage not only the requirements on our part, but as well, what the Lord is doing for the believer.

The question could be asked, Does the phrase insinuate that there are some believers who do not love God? No, that's not the idea. The idea of the text is that all believers in fact do love God. Actually, it would be impossible for a believer not to do so (providing he is a true believer), and for the reason that believers at the moment of conversion have the divine nature imparted unto them. To the degree of that love, however, is something else again.

TO THEM WHO ARE THE CALLED
ACCORDING TO HIS PURPOSE

The heading proclaims the second qualification. Our lives must be for His purpose, and not our purpose, and here is where the great conflict begins.

The working of the Holy Spirit in our lives sent to us to carry out the will of God pertains here to the calling of which the apostle speaks. It is twofold:

1. It is the calling as it pertains to the everlasting purpose of God, which was ordained before the foundations of the world were laid.

2. As we have previously stated, this calling concerns a personal objective, even as it is a part of the whole.

That spoken is the effort being carried out by the Holy Spirit, and it is our business to see to it that His purpose is our purpose as well. Unfortunately, the terrible struggle of self-will enters in here, which greatly hinders the Holy Spirit and presents a conflict to the believer that is not easily overcome. The flesh is so subtle that most of the time it masquerades under great spiritual claims. It takes total consecration on the part of the believer in order for the Holy Spirit to point out these areas of spiritual weakness, which we sometimes think in our delusion are great spiritual strengths. In fact, it is a lifelong struggle. However, the Lord does not require perfection in this area, simply because were that the case none would qualify. He does require love for Himself, and that portrays the direction of our hearts.

Wuest said, in that view, the text literally reads, "And we know with an absolute knowledge that all things are constantly working together, resulting in good for those who are loving God, for those who are called ones according to His purpose."

Having these qualities of love for God, and our calling being according to His purpose and not our own, all things then must work together for our good, and in fact do work together for our good.

FOR WHOM HE DID FOREKNOW

"For whom He did foreknow, He also did predestinate to be conformed to the image of His Son, that He might be the firstborn among many brethren" (Rom. 8:29).

If the preacher is not pointing people to the Cross, what he is saying is a waste of time. The only solution in fact, for mankind, is the Cross of Christ.

God is omniscient, meaning that He knows everything—past, present, and future. Consequently, foreknowledge is His ability to look down through time in whatever capacity or to whatever degree, and therefore see and know what will take place at that particular time and with whomever it involves.

It is true that the Scripture makes use of anthropomorphic (related in human terms) forms of expression regarding the way in which God obtains knowledge (Gen. 3:8), and sometimes even represents Him as if He did not know certain things (Gen. 11:5; 18:21); nevertheless the constant representation of the Scripture is that God knows everything. This perfect knowledge of God, moreover, is not merely a knowledge that is practically unlimited for all spiritual purposes, but covers every aspect of all things in the strictest sense of the term.

In the historical books of the Old Testament, the omniscience of God is a constant underlying presupposition when it is said that God watches men's actions, knows their acts and words, and discloses to them the future; while in the psalms, prophets and wisdom books, this divine attribute becomes an object of reflection, and finds doctrinal expression.

ALWAYS HAS BEEN

It cannot, however, be said that this attribute of God—the knowing of all things—appears only late in the history of special revelation; it is a characteristic of the biblical idea of God from the very first, and it is only its expression that comes out with special clearness in the later books. God's knowledge then is represented as perfect. Since He is free from all limits of space, His omniscience is frequently connected with His omnipresence (He is everywhere).

GOD IS NOT BOUND BY TIME RESTRAINTS

God is also, according to the Old Testament, free from all limitations of time, so that His consciousness is not in the midst of the stream of the succeeding moments of time, as is the case with the human consciousness.

God is not only without beginning or end of days, but with Him a thousand years are as one day or vice versa. Hence, God knows in one eternal intuition that which for the human consciousness is past, present, and future. In a strict sense, therefore, regarding the foreknowledge of God, and the distinction in God's knowledge which we derive from His Word, such is actually the only way in which we can conceive of divine omniscience in its relation to time, and our understanding of such.

GOD'S KNOWLEDGE OF EVENTS

It is God's knowledge of events, which from the human point of view is future that constitutes His foreknowledge in the sense of that which we understand, or attempt to understand.

God is represented as having a knowledge of the entire course of events before they take place. Such knowledge belongs to the supernatural power of God from the very outset of special revelation.

He knows beforehand what Abraham will do, and what will happen to him; He knows beforehand that Pharaoh's heart will be hardened, and that Moses will deliver Israel (Gen. 15:13; Ex. 3:19; 7:4; 11:1). Actually, the entire history of this period of revelation exhibits plainly the foreknowledge of God in this sense.

PROPHECY

Prophecy, which makes up about one-third of the Bible, is actually the foreknowledge of God. This means that nothing future is hidden from Jehovah (Isa. 41:22; 42:9; 43:9–13; 44:6–8; 46:10; Dan. 2:22; Amos 3:7), and this foreknowledge embraces the entire course of man's life, whoever that man may be (Ps. 31:15; 39:5; 139:4–6, 16; Job 14:5).

Passages from Isaiah show that it is from the occurrence of events in accordance with Jehovah's predictions that the prophet will prove His foreknowledge; and that in contrast with the worshipers of idols which are taken by surprise (in other words, they don't know what is coming), Israel is warned of the future by the omniscient Jehovah.

THE NEW TESTAMENT

In the New Testament likewise, God's omniscience is explicitly affirmed. Jesus taught that God knows the hidden secrets of man's heart (Lk. 16:15); and this is also the teaching of the apostles (Acts 1:24; 15:8; I Cor. 2:10; 3:20; I Thess. 2:4; Rev. 2:23).

In a word, according to the author of the epistle to the Hebrews, whom I think was Paul, everything is open to God, so that He is literally omniscient, i.e., all-knowing (Heb. 4:13).

Actually, Jesus asserts a foreknowledge by God of that which is hidden from the Son, at least was hidden at that time (Mk. 13:32), and James asserts that all God's works are foreknown by Him (Acts 15:18).

DOES GOD'S FOREKNOWLEDGE
IMPACT FREE WILL?

Denials of the divine foreknowledge have been occasioned by the supposed conflict of this truth with human freedom, in other words, free will and choice on the part of man. It was supposed that in order to be free, an event must be uncertain and contingent as regards the fact of its future happening, and in the most absolute sense, that is, from the Divine as well as the human point of view. Hence, there have been many in the past who have denied the foreknowledge of God.

It was supposed either that God voluntarily determines not to foresee the free volitions of man, or else that since God's omniscience is simply the knowledge of all that is knowable, it does not embrace the free acts of man which are by their very nature uncertain and consequently, unknowable, at least they say. Upon this view of freedom, this denial of God's foreknowledge was logically necessary.

Of course, to take that view, one has to come to the erroneous conclusion, that God has created all things, and merely sits by as an onlooker regarding the course of all events be they present or future, and which are necessarily entirely independent of His purpose and control; however, if anyone reads the Bible at all, we know this thinking has no place in Scripture, considering that God is involved in everything.

If God foreknows future events as certain, then they must be certain, and if so, then the certainty of their actually occurring must depend either upon God's decree and providential control, or else upon a fate independent of God. This we know is not the case, and in fact cannot be the case.

TO WHAT EXTENT?

It has been the thinking of some that God has a knowledge of events as conditionally future, that is, events neither merely possible nor certainly future, but suspended upon conditions undetermined by God. However, this is not true. Besides being contrary to the Scripture in its idea that many events lie outside the decree of God, and that God must wait upon man in His government of the world, there is really no such class of events as this theory asserts. As we have already stated, God is involved in everything.

If God foreknows that the conditions on which they are suspended will be fulfilled, then these events belong to the class of events that are certainly future. If God does not know whether or not the conditions will be fulfilled by man, then His foreknowledge is denied and these events in question belong to the class of the happenstance. The Scripture passages to which appeal is made to try to buttress such a doctrine such as Genesis 11:6; Exodus 3:19; Deuteronomy 7:3–4; I Samuel 23:10–13; II Samuel 12:8, etc., do not afford a basis for this doctrine.

The Scripture recognizes that God has put all things in particular categories, and speaks of what can or cannot happen under such and such conditions; however, none of these passages assert or imply that the events are suspended upon conditions that are either unknown or undetermined or not controlled by God.

GOD'S PLAN

God's foreknowledge, according to the Scripture, is based upon His plan or eternal purpose, which embraces everything that comes to pass. God is never represented as a mere onlooker seeing the future course of events, but having no part in them. That God has such a plan is the teaching of the entire scope of Scripture. It is implied in the Old Testament conception of God as an omnipotent (all-powerful) person governing all things in accordance with His divine plan.

This idea is involved in the names of God revealed to the patriarchs: El, Elohim, El Shaddai, and in the prophetic name, Jehovah of Hosts. This latter name teaches not only God's infinite power and glory, but also makes Him known as interposing in accordance with His sovereign will and purpose in the affairs of this world, and as having also the spiritual powers of the heavenly world at His disposal for the execution of His eternal purpose. Hence, the idea of God comes to signify the omnipotent ruler of the universe (Ps. 24:10; Isa. 6:3; 51:5; 54:5; Jer. 10:16; Amos 9:5).

HUMAN HISTORY

Not only in this conception of God as omnipotent and sovereign ruler is the thought of His eternal plan evolved, it is explicitly asserted throughout the whole Old Testament. The purpose of God as determining human history in the book of Genesis lies clearly upon the surface of the narrative, as, for example, in the history of Abraham and of Joseph.

Where there is no abstract statement of this truth, it is evident that the writer regards every event as but the unfolding of the purposes and plan of God. In the psalms, prophets, and wisdom books, this truth finds explicit and reiterated assertion. Jehovah has an eternal purpose (Ps. 33:11), and this purpose will certainly come to pass (Isa. 14:27; 43:13).

As well, this purpose includes all events and renders certain their occurrence (Isa. 14:24; 40:10; 46:9–10; Zech. 1:6).

Also, the providential control wherewith Jehovah executes this plan includes the heart of man (Prov. 21:1).

Likewise and stated, the New Testament regards all history as but the unfolding of God's eternal purpose (Acts 4:28), which includes man's salvation (Eph. 1:4–5; II Tim. 1:9), the provision of Christ as Saviour (I Pet. 1:20), and the character and nature of the Christian (Eph. 2:10). In other words, God is able to do all things without interfering with man's free moral agency, and because He is truly omniscient, omnipotent, and omnipresent.

SO HOW DO WE ANSWER ALL THE QUESTIONS WHICH GOD'S FOREKNOWLEDGE PROPOSES?

Knowing and understanding that God is involved in every single event of human history, even to a far greater degree than our human minds can grasp, how are certain things reconciled? If one is to consider that the Lord notes every sparrow's fall, and numbers the hairs on each and every head of every person in the world (Mat. 10:29–30), then one has at least some idea as to the degree of involvement. As stated, it is beyond comprehension.

So how can God have this much involvement, foreknow-ing all things and, at the same time, not impact the free will of man? This we do know concerning man's free will: while God speaks to men, deals with men, moves upon men, and convicts and even pressures men, there is no record in the Word of God that He violates the free moral agency (free will) of any person. Actually, the entirety of the tone and tint of Scripture is *"who-soever will"* (Rev. 22:17).

The only answer that one can give in respect to this question is that God, who has and who is divine power, divine knowl-edge and divine presence, can involve Himself in anything desired and to any degree desired, and, at the same time, not affect man's free moral agency, at least to go beyond the normal appeal. Still, in every sense of the word, once a certain level is reached, God is beyond the comprehension of man. He wouldn't be God were that not the case.

HE ALSO DID PREDESTINATE

The heading proclaims here the basic Bible teaching of predestination, which deals with God's plan. However, predestination does not pertain to individual conformity of free wills to that plan. God has called all men and all are free to accept or reject the call (Jn. 3:16; I Tim. 2:4; II Pet. 3:9; Rev. 22:17).

All who do accept He has foreknown and predestinated to be conformed to the image of His Son that His Son might be the firstborn among many brethren. Those who reject the plan He has foreknown and predestinated to be consigned to eternal hell as an everlasting monument of His wrath against those who oppose His will (Isa. 66:22–24; Rev. 14:9–11; Mat. 25:41, 46).

PREDESTINATION AS A DOCTRINE

As is known, there are several views on this subject, with the view I have just given being that of this writer. Many in the church world subscribe to the Calvinistic view of predestination. They believe that it is the aspect of foreordination whereby the salvation of the believer is taken to be effected in accordance with the will of God, who has called and elected him in Christ unto life eternal. In other words, the individual has nothing to do with his or her eternal destination, with that having been decided by God from eternity past, or so it is believed by those who subscribe to this particular doctrine. However, this same teaching concludes that while God has elected some for salvation, that there is nothing taught in Scripture that points to personal reprobation. In other words, they teach that God has predestined some to be eternally lost, i.e., consigned to the lake of fire forever. However, to believe one is to believe the other. It is impossible to have it both ways.

If God has elected certain persons for salvation, then simply by not being elected automatically consigns them to eternal darkness, or so they say.

CALVIN

Calvin's view of predestination, which we believe to be rank error, had a strange way of addressing this problem. He said,

"Man therefore falls, God's Providence so ordaining, but he falls by his own fault."

That statement is a contradiction in terms. How could he fall by his own fault if God had so ordained it?

The argument may well be made, which it seems that Calvin tried to make, that God ordained the fall only to the extent that through foreknowledge He knew it would happen.

However, once again the problem of contradiction arises. If God ordained the fall, then man has no choice in the matter.

It is true that God has ordained, even as Romans 8:29 proclaims, that if man falls through his own free will, he will be eternally lost. (Fall is here used in the sense of dying lost.)

AUGUSTINE

Augustine lived about 400 years after Christ and was called by some the "father of theology."

In his teaching on the absolute will of God, he made divine grace the only grounds for man's salvation. It was to him the irresistible power working faith within the heart, and bringing freedom as its result.

He was partly right. Divine grace is the only grounds for man's salvation (Eph. 2:8–9). However, grace cannot be an irresistible power, for in so doing it would cease to be grace. As grace is a free gift of God, it must be freely offered, and the entire scope of Scripture maintains that if it is grace it must be freely received.

Evidently, Augustine was attempting to reconcile the plain teaching of the Word of God respecting grace with an erroneous view of predestination. Calvin's teaching on predestination simply carried the Augustinian theory to its logical and necessary conclusion, and he was the first to adopt the doctrine as the cardinal point of a theological system.

Calvin's mode of defining predestination is that such is the eternal decree of God, by which He has decided with Himself what is to become of each and every individual. All, he maintained, are not created in like condition, but eternal life is foreordained for some, and eternal condemnation for others.

However, even Calvin confessed that his view of predestination was a "horrible decree." Yet he somehow maintained that it was love—"the fatherly love of God," as he termed it—the efficiency of saving love—which fueled these decisions. (Calvin lived in the 16th century.)

Predestination is a biblical doctrine if understood correctly. It simply means that certain situations are predestined by God, but whoever would be involved in those plans is not predestined. For instance, it is predestined that Louisiana State University is going to have a football team. Who makes the team is not predestined.

THE DOCTRINE OF UNCONDITIONAL
ETERNAL SECURITY

From the teaching of Augustine and Calvin came the unscriptural doctrine of unconditional eternal security. In brief, this teaching claims that once a believer is saved he cannot be lost, irrespective of what he may do or how much he may lose his faith, etc. However, most advocates of this doctrine differ from Augustine and Calvin in that man is saved not because he is predestined to be so, but because of his own free will.

This doctrine, as far as I am concerned, is dishonest in that it embraces part of Calvinism, while rejecting the rest.

Both doctrines have caused untold millions, I feel, to die eternally lost. If it is already predestined, then one should not even be concerned about one's soul, knowing that what will be, will be. As well, all evangelism stops respecting predestination. What's the point? Those who are going to be saved will be saved, and those who are not going to be saved won't be saved, irrespective in either case of what anyone does or doesn't do. Some have attempted to address this glaring conclusion by claiming that while it already has been decided, still those who are saved must work very hard to bring in the others; however, that is only a salve attempting to address the gross error.

Once again, if it is already predestined, what difference does it make as to how hard one works to bring others to Christ; it's all a moot point. Likewise it is the same with unconditional eternal security. Untold millions have been taught that they could lose their faith, cease to believe, and still be saved.

ARMINIUS

Jacob Arminius lived in the late 16th century. He strongly opposed Calvin's teaching on predestination. It is his interpretation of the Scriptures respecting this subject, to which we basically subscribe.

Arminianism gives grace a supreme place and makes it, when welcomed, pass into saving grace. The idea of that statement is simply that it is by grace that one is saved (Eph. 2:8–9). However, it is only when grace is welcomed and accepted that it then becomes saving grace. In other words, the grace of God is abundant to all, but can only be extended to those *"whosoever will"* (Rev. 22:17).

He made election depend on faith, which is the condition of universal grace. This statement means that God has elected people to be saved who exhibit faith in His Son, the Lord Jesus Christ, and the sacrifice He gave of Himself at Calvary. While grace is universal, meaning free to all, as it must be if it is to be grace, the condition for receiving grace is, as stated, "faith."

THE SIGNIFICANCE OF THESE DOCTRINES

Arminianism rejects the so-called elect grace of the predestination theory. This teaches that grace is extended only to those who are predestined to be saved. Of course, the Bible teaches no such thing. It does teach *"whosoever will"* (Rev. 22:17).

Arminianism holds that the awakened human will to cooperate with divine grace in such wise that it rests with the human will, whether the divine grace is really accepted or rejected.

Arminianism looks to faith and repentance as conditions of personal salvation (Acts 20:21). The Arminian standpoint admits the foreknowledge of God but denies foreordination (some ordained to be saved and some ordained to be lost).

The reader may think these doctrines to be of little significance; however, to be blunt, there are untold millions at this moment in hell simply because they had an erroneous view of these subjects as it concerned their soul's salvation. No, these doctrines are not of small consequence, but rather the very opposite. The believer should know what he believes and why he believes it. We teach, as stated, that it is faith that gets one into salvation—faith in Christ and what He did for us at the Cross. Likewise, it is faith that keeps us in. The only thing that can cause a believer to lose his soul is to quit believing; in other words, the person no longer exhibits faith in Christ and what Christ has done at the Cross. Such a person then resorts to the position of being an unbeliever, which means the loss of the soul, that is, if the person continues in that capacity.

Sin, as hurtful and harmful as it is, will not cause a believer to lose his or her soul. That in no way is meant to condone sin. It is not sin but rather a lack of faith that can cause a person to lose his soul.

There are millions who claim to be saved and living a life of debauchery with never any repentance in sight, but they think they are saved because someone tells them they are. Please remember, the Lord saves *from* sin, not *in* sin. So these millions, sad to say, are not saved. In fact, they've never been saved.

TO BE CONFORMED TO THE IMAGE OF HIS SON

The heading presents the predestination addressed here, and the only predestination addressed.

Those, who of their own free will, accept Christ are predestined to be conformed by the Holy Spirit into the Christlike image, which we have been addressing here throughout the entirety of this chapter.

Let us observe the way in which Paul introduces this subject so as to better understand his drift.

He has been speaking of the trials and imperfections of the present life and urging his readers not to be discouraged by them on the grounds that if they continue to "live after the Spirit," these things will by no means hinder, but rather further the final issue. To strengthen this position, he introduces the thought of God's eternal purpose.

The idea is that the believer is in the state of grace in which he now finds himself, having accepted it, due to God's eternal purpose to call him to this state.

Consequently, it is impossible that the circumstances in which He has placed us, or any power thereafter, should thwart His purpose, providing we continue to believe Him.

In the Greek, the word *conformed* is *summorphos*, and it means "to be made like unto." So the idea is that the believer become Christlike in every way. Hence, He said, *"learn of Me"* (Mat. 11:29).

In the Greek, the word *image* is *eikon*, and means "a copy, representation, or resemblance."

THAT HE MIGHT BE THE FIRSTBORN AMONG MANY BRETHREN

The heading doesn't mean that Jesus was born again as a sinner, as some teach, but rather that He is the father of the salvation plan, having paid the price on the Cross, which made it all possible.

Some have tried to use the word *firstborn,* as it referred to our Lord, as becoming a sinner on the Cross, and then born again in hell of all places. Of course, there is not a shred of scriptural evidence to back that up.

Jesus did not become a sinner on the Cross. Had He done so, then He could not have presented Himself as a perfect sacrifice. In fact, He became a sin offering (Isa. 53:10). Jesus didn't go to the Cross to become a sinner; He went to the Cross because He was to be and was the Saviour. He atoned for all sin on the Cross by giving Himself as a perfect sacrifice. His spirit, soul, and body had to be perfect for it to be accepted by God, which it was. So, when the Holy Spirit used the word *firstborn,* referring to our Lord, He was referring to Him as being the father of the salvation plan, as stated, having paid the price on the Cross, which made it all possible.

(The author is indebted to Caspar Wistar Hodge for excerpts from his insights on foreknowledge.)

Saviour, again to Thy dear name we raise,
With one accord, our parting hymn of praise;
We stand to bless Thee ere our worship cease,
Then lowly kneeling, wait Thy word of peace.

Grant us Thy peace upon our homeward way;
With Thee began, with Thee shall end the day;
Guard Thou the lips from sin, the hearts from shame,
That in this house have called upon Thy name.

Grant us Thy peace, Lord, through the coming night,
Turn Thou for us its darkness into light,
From harm and danger keep Thy children free,
For dark and light are both alike to Thee.

Grant us Thy peace throughout our earthly life,
Our balm in sorrow, and our stay in strife;
Then, when Thy voice shall bid our conflict cease,
Call us, O Lord, to Thine eternal peace.

How The Holy Spirit Works

CHAPTER 10

PREDESTINATION

PREDESTINATION

"MOREOVER WHOM HE DID predestinate, them He also called: And whom He called, them He also justified, and whom He justified, them He also glorified" (Rom. 8:30).

MOREOVER WHOM HE DID PREDESTINATE

Except for the Cross, every human being on earth would be eternally lost. The Cross opened the door for every good thing to be given to humanity, at least for those who will believe.

The heading does not refer to some predestinated to be lost and others to be saved, but rather refers back to Romans 8:29, in that those who accept Him of their own freewill He has predestinated them *"to be conformed to the image of His Son."*

The promise of *"whosoever will"* runs like a deep river all the way from the book of Genesis through the book of Revelation. Actually, the first invitation was given in the garden of Eden immediately after the fall when *"the LORD God called unto Adam and said unto him, Where are you?"* (Gen. 3:9). It closes out in the book of Revelation with such an appeal that no one need misunderstand what is being said.

As well, understanding that these were among the last words given by the Holy Spirit as He closed out the canon of Scripture, there need not be any misunderstanding as to His intentions. Actually, it is the only time in the Bible that the Holy Spirit refers to Himself as speaking, and says, *"and the Spirit and the bride say, Come. And let him who hears say, Come. And let him who is athirst come. And whosoever will, let him take the water of life freely"* (Rev. 22:17).

As well, in between those great beginning and ending books of the Bible, the words of Jesus echo to the whole of humanity when He said, *"if any man thirst, let him come unto Me and drink"* (Jn. 7:37). If one is to notice, He said, "any man," and He meant exactly what He said, which means the invitation is not extended to only a few who are predestinated. In fact, and as we have said, if men are already predestinated for heaven, what's the point of the invitation anyway?

THEM HE ALSO CALLED

First of all, and it should be settled, God has called, even as I think we have adequately illustrated, the whole of humanity, and for all time. If salvation is available to one, then it must be available to all. As stated, that's the warp and woof of the entirety of the Bible: *"whosoever will."* That means there is no such thing as a limited atonement, a limited salvation, or a limited call for that matter (Jn. 3:16; 7:37).

Actually, God has to call in order for anyone to be saved. Man is so spiritually dead that on his own he does not, and in fact cannot call upon God. With no spiritual life in him and dead in trespasses and sins (Eph. 2:1), this means he is dead to all things that pertain to God. Therefore, no human being in his sinful, unconverted, unregenerate state has ever called on God without the Holy Spirit first of all in some manner awakening him to his need. As stated, that call is going out to the whole of humanity, and has for all time.

FOREKNOWLEDGE

This is done despite the fact that God through foreknowledge knows who is going to accept and who is going to reject. Nevertheless, in respect to those who reject, when they stand at the great white throne judgment (Rev. 20:11-15), they will not be able to say that they had no opportunity. Paul makes that abundantly clear in Romans 1:20.

About a thousand years before Christ, the Holy Spirit through Solomon said, *"Turn you at My reproof* (repent): *behold* (if you will do this), *I will pour out My Spirit unto you, I will make known My words unto you. Because I have called, and you refused; I have stretched out My hand, and no man regarded; but you have set at nought all My counsel, and would none of My reproof: I also will laugh at your calamity; I will mock when your fear comes"* (Prov. 1:23-26).

Predestination erroneously thought and claims that all who are called accept. However, the Word of God is clear and plain that all who are called do not accept. In fact, only a few do (Mat. 7:13-14).

As this call is given to something, rather someone; it is also given for something: to be conformed to the image of His Son. The sinner is called from something to something—in this case, from darkness to light, from sin to salvation, from lost to found, from hell to heaven, from spiritual death to spiritual life, from Satan to Jesus, etc.

AND WHOM HE CALLED, THEM HE ALSO JUSTIFIED

The heading means that God takes away the guilt and penalty for sins and bestows upon the believing sinner a positive righteousness, even Jesus Christ Himself, in whom the believer now stands forever innocent, uncondemned, and righteous in every point of law.

This speaks of the moral law of Moses, which, in reality, is the law of God and is incumbent upon every human being who has ever lived. It cannot change because it is moral law, therefore it stands forever. Again I speak of the Ten Commandments, minus the fourth which was not carried over into the new covenant because it, of all the ten, was not moral but rather ceremonial and fulfilled in Christ.

In fact, all of the commandments are fulfilled in Christ. As our representative man, He kept every commandment in totality, never violating even one in word, thought, or deed. Upon our acceptance of Him, and our faith registered in Him and what

He did for us at the Cross, we are given the perfection of Christ, meaning that instead of being lawbreakers, which carries the penalty of eternal spiritual death, we are now lawkeepers, all because of Christ and what He did for us at the Cross.

AND WHOM HE JUSTIFIED, THEM HE ALSO GLORIFIED

The heading refers to the act of God yet to come, which will transform the believer's body at the rapture (resurrection) into a body like the resurrected body of our Lord Jesus Christ. As stated, this is a future event, yet the apostle puts it in the past tense. How can he do this?

The Holy Spirit through Paul said these words in this way because in the mind of God it is a guaranteed event, although future. Actually, only God can guarantee future events. The idea is that just as surely as the believer has been justified, he will just as surely be glorified.

The whole argument of Romans 6-8 has been that justification and the new life of holiness in the Spirit are inseparable experiences. Hence, Paul can take one step to the end and write, *"and whom He justified, them He also glorified."* Yet, the tense in the last word is amazing.

THE MOST DARING ANTICIPATION OF FAITH

It has been said that this particular phrase from Romans 8:30 is the most daring anticipation of faith found in the entirety of the New Testament. As well, the life is not to be taken out of it by the philosophical consideration that with God there is neither before nor after. The glorification as stated is already consummated, though still future in the fullest sense.

The idea is this: the step implied in *"He also glorified,"* is both complete and certain in the divine counsels.

The Holy Spirit is explaining here the totality of salvation. As such, He does it as only it can be done by proclaiming its totality. Consequently, even though the saint does not yet have the last step of glorification, its certitude is as sure as God. He has already decreed it; therefore, the resurrection is certain (the resurrection will be the time of glorification).

In fact, Jesus is the resurrection. When Martha said unto Him, *"Lord, if you had been here, my brother had not died,"* Jesus said unto her, *"Your brother shall rise again."*

Martha understood that to refer to the coming resurrection of all saints and answered accordingly. However, Jesus said unto her, *"I am the resurrection and the life."*

In other words, He said to her, "Martha, look at Me. You are looking at the resurrection. I am the resurrection and the life" (Jn. 11:20-26).

WHAT SHALL WE THEN SAY TO THESE THINGS?

"What shall we then say to these things? If God be for us, who can be against us?" (Rom. 8:31).

The Cross of Christ is the only solution for sin. Any claim other than Jesus Christ and Him crucified is bogus.

The question presented in the heading is meant to take the believer far above the difficulties of this present time. In other words, looking to that coming day, the resurrection, when all things will then be made right.

The two words—these things—refer to the suffering presently endured (Rom. 8:17-18) in comparison with *"the glory which shall be revealed in us."* The apostle has disparaged the suffering in comparison with the glory. He has interpreted it as in a manner prophetic of the glory (Rom. 8:19-27).

Romans 8:31 refers to what we, as believers, have to go through here in this present life. Irrespective of the difficulties and the problems, whatever they might be and as severe as they might be, mean nothing in the light of eternity. We should always understand that, and never get our eyes off of the future and onto the present.

IF GOD BE FOR US, WHO CAN BE AGAINST US?

The question of the heading puts everything in its proper perspective.

In the Greek, the word *if* is *ei*, and it means "a fulfilled condition." Consequently, if should have been translated, "Since God is for us." As well, the words "be" and "can be" are in italics in your Bible, which means that they are not in the original Greek text, but were supplied by the translators in an effort to fill out the thought.

The thought of Paul is not in the form of a hypothetical condition, as if it were a question as to whether God is for us or not. Wuest said Paul's thought was this: "In view of the fact that God is for us, who is or could be against us so as to do us harm? That is, since God is for the saints, on our side, who can harm us?"

HE WHO SPARED NOT HIS OWN SON

"He who spared not His own Son, but delivered Him up for us all, how shall He not with Him also freely give us all things?" (Rom. 8:32).

As far as we know, the Cross of Christ is the very first doctrine formulated by the Godhead. It was formulated before the foundation of the world (I Pet. 1:18-20).

The heading concerns the great gift of God, the Lord Jesus Christ. In the Greek, the word *spared* is *pheidomai*, and it means "to treat leniently, to spare." The idea is that God did not treat His Son leniently or spare Him. He gave heaven's best.

The idea is that there was never any question that love would do this thing, because love must redeem, at least if it is possible. The tremendous cost and price were ever before God.

BUT DELIVERED HIM UP FOR US ALL

The heading concerns the whole of mankind and not just a select, predestined few.

Delivered Him up to what? He delivered Him up to become a man, the form of which incidentally, He will retain forever, and of course we're speaking of the Lord Jesus Christ.

That within itself is altogether beyond anything that we could even begin to think. What He was, the Creator of the Ages, *"dwelling in the light which no man can approach unto; whom no man has seen, nor can see,"* is beyond our comprehension (I Tim. 6:16).

For 33 and one-half years He lived as a peasant, and during His three and one-half years of public ministry, He was reviled, scorned, rejected, and then crucified.

All of that was one thing, but the bearing of the sin penalty for all of mankind was an act that was absolutely unselfish, to say the least. The word *unselfish* is totally inadequate to describe Him. What He had to do to redeem man was so awful that even God could not look upon the scene. This portrays that which no other human being has ever experienced.

Even though He now resides in a glorified body and will do so forever, still, that is a far cry from what He once had but will never have again, due to what He did for humanity. He did it for sinners. He did it for those who did not love Him.

HOW SHALL HE NOT WITH HIM ALSO FREELY GIVE US ALL THINGS?

The heading lays bare before believers the tremendous price paid for our redemption. The idea is that if God has done this—the giving up of His only Son in order that we might be saved—how can we think that He is going to allow us to be overcome by the Evil One, and I speak of those who truly want to live for God.

This does not mean that God will keep one against His will, but it does mean that irrespective of what comes or goes, those who want to live for God irrespective of the opposition need not fear. If the Lord did what He did respecting our salvation, then one can be certain that He will do whatever it takes to keep that for which so much has been paid.

George Williams said:

"These things being so, if God being for us, who can be against us so as to injure us? As well, believers need not be anxious, for God being for us fills the heart with a rest and a peace that shuts out all anxiety as to anything that could trouble it; for how could the heart and the hand that gave what was most precious to them fail in bounty, liberality, and protection to those whom He has saved?"

HE WHO HAS DONE SO MUCH IS
CERTAIN TO DO MUCH MORE

Wuest says, "In the first phrase of the Scripture, 'His own' in the Greek is 'idios,' and means 'one's own peculiar private possession.' Our Lord is the Father's very own private possession, infinitely dear to Him."

In the Greek, the word *freely* is *dorean* and means "without a cost, freely, gratuitously." God freely gives us that which is most precious to His—His Son.

In other words, God gives us all things, not because we deserve them, but in reality we deserve the very opposite. He does it because of His love and His grace. In other words, it is done not because of merit and neither is it expecting anything in return. It is a gift.

The phrase, *"He not with Him,"* speaks of both God the Father and God the Son working in conjunction to bring about this great redemption. They are also working to give us divine protection and, as well, a guarantee that everything that goes with salvation, such as glorification, will ultimately come.

WHO SHALL LAY ANYTHING TO THE CHARGE OF GOD'S ELECT?

"Who shall lay anything to the charge of God's elect? It is God who justifies" (Rom. 8:33).

The Cross of Christ is God's answer to man's dilemma. If the Cross of Christ is taken out of the gospel, there really remains no gospel.

The heading in effect means, "Who shall pronounce those guilty whom God pronounces righteous?"

This means that every single sin that has ever been committed by the trusting believer has been washed away by the precious shed blood of Jesus Christ, and it was because of one's faith in that shed blood.

As someone has well said, "The Christian has no past, and Satan has no future!"

This means that it is terribly improper and actually an insult to God for a believer to bring up the sins of another that have long since been washed clean by the blood of Jesus. As well, it is insulting to the Lord for the believer to drag out his own sins again—sins that the Lord has already forgiven. It does such a terrible injustice to the mercy and grace of God, considering that God does much more than merely forgive. He not only forgives, but He actually erases the sin from the account of the believer, consequently, treating him as if the infraction was never committed. Actually, that is what justification means. The sin is not only forgiven, it is stricken from the record, and as far as God is concerned, it was never committed.

IT IS GOD WHO JUSTIFIES

The heading means that no one, not even Satan or his evil angels, dare question or deny God's great plan of justification.

Wuest said, "Even God cannot do both, accuse and justify, at the same time. And since our justification resides in a person, the Lord Jesus our righteousness, in whom we stand as uncondemned and unchargeable, even as the Son Himself, it is impossible, after having been justified, that we be again accused—and brought under condemnation."

In the Greek, the word *elect* is *eklektos*, and means "chosen out ones." Paul's argument is, "Who shall prefer any charge or accusation against the chosen-out ones of God?"

WHAT DOES *ELECT* MEAN?

God's purpose is to save all who conform to His plan—and this is His choice or election in the matter. By grace, men who conform will become the elect and be saved, while those who do not will be damned (Mk. 16:15-16; Lk. 13:1-5; Jn. 3:16-18; I Tim. 2:4-5; II Pet. 3:9; Rev. 22:17).

The choice was first on God's part, but it must be accepted by men for them to receive the benefits and become a part of the elect or chosen ones of God (Jn. 15:16; Eph. 1:4; 2:10; II Thess. 2:13). Men must make their calling and election sure, as stated in II Peter 1:10.

It is scripturally erroneous to think that God has elected some people to be lost and some people to be saved, as some teach. Furthermore, according to this erroneous teaching, there is absolutely nothing they can do about their place or status. They are either doomed to die eternally lost and they cannot stop it, or they are destined to go to heaven, which will happen no matter what they do. Such false doctrine—and false it is—is not taught in the Word of God.

The truth is this: As the gospel is preached, anyone who will accept the Lord—irrespective as to whom he or she might be—immediately becomes *"God's elect"* (Jn. 15:16; Rom. 8:33; Titus 1:1). Satan has caused many to be lost because they have believed the lie that they are elected to be lost.

Let us say it again: There could be nothing further from the truth. The Scripture still says, and always will, *"whosoever will..."* (Rev. 22:17).

ELECTION FOR A SPECIAL PURPOSE

Election in this capacity, which happens constantly, is the act of choice whereby God picks an individual or group out of a larger company for a purpose or destiny of his own appointment. The main Old Testament word in the Hebrew for this is the verb *beahar*, which expresses the idea of deliberately selecting someone or something after carefully considering the alternatives. The word implies a decided preference.

The reason that God does this is known only to Him. Having perfect knowledge, He looks at a believer and chooses that believer on the basis of what He knows that believer can and will be in Him.

That means that every single preacher of the gospel has, in a sense, been elected by God for this particular task with God, of course, knowing all that each preacher would be and do at the time of his calling. So He called David anyway, knowing that David would fail miserably in the case of Bathsheba and her husband Uriah. In fact, He chose Israel, knowing they would fail and even crucify His own beloved Son. This did not come as a surprise to the Lord.

WHY WOULD GOD, KNOWING THERE WOULD BE FAILURE, ELECT SOMEONE?

First of all, if we judge anything by its present appearance, we are judging wrong.

Anything and everything that God has elected will ultimately come out to the good. In other words, Israel will one day be totally and completely restored. However, it will be at the time of their own volition and as they make a choice to accept Jesus Christ as their Messiah and Saviour. Admittedly, all of those who lived through the many centuries of rebellion and rejection will be and are eternally lost. Nevertheless, Israel will ultimately come back, even as God has known all along that they will.

Despite the fact of the apostate church and lukewarmness, there is a remnant—as there has always been a remnant—who loves God and serves Him. They do it of their own choice freely and willingly loving Him out of their heart, which has to be of free will or it simply cannot be love. In that case, it is *"a glorious church"* (Eph. 5:27).

WHO IS HE WHO CONDEMNS?

"Who is he who condemns? It is Christ who died, yea rather who is risen again, who is even at the right hand of God, who also makes intercession for us" (Rom. 8:34).

The Cross will ultimately make everything come out right, at least for those who love the Lord. Actually, the entirety of Christianity, at least the part of Christianity that abides by the Word, is centered up in the Cross.

The question of the heading is very similar to the question of the previous verse, but with one difference.

The climax of this chapter is now reached, and the apostle triumphantly challenges anyone to lay anything to the charge of God's elect. This glorious word *elect* first occurs here in this epistle. The expiatory character of Christ's death is affirmed in verse 34 and the meaning of justification in verse 33. The challenge, *"Who shall lay* (bring) *anything to the charge of* (a charge against) *God's elect?"* i.e., who shall pronounce those guilty whom God pronounces righteous, makes clear its significance.

The only one who dares to condemn the child of God, especially considering what Jesus Christ has done for Him and the price that He paid is Satan and his followers. The Scripture labels him as the *"accuser of our* (the) *brethren"* (Rev. 12:10).

Consequently, when a believer stoops to the low, low level of accusing or condemning another believer, such accusers have joined in the league of Satan and have actually entered into a form of witchcraft. This is especially true if that believer who has failed has thrown himself on the grace and mercy of the Lord and is trying with all of his strength to follow the Lord despite the failure of the past.

WHAT DOES PAUL MEAN
BY THE WORD *CONDEMN?*

Condemnation is an important concept. It is important both theologically and spiritually, for there are many persons whose sense of guilt leads them to fear condemnation. It is important even for those who need not fear condemnation, for too often Christians are tempted to take God's place and judge (condemn) others.

THE OLD TESTAMENT CONCEPT

The Hebrew word *rasha* is usually translated "condemn." It means "to be wicked or act wickedly."

Another word, *asam,* which means "to offend," or "to be guilty," is also infrequently translated, "to condemn," or "to be condemned." The thought is that the person who chooses a wicked rather than a godly lifestyle has brought himself or herself under condemnation.

It is important to remember that the wicked can turn from their ways (Ezek. 18) and that repentance and confession can restore a right relationship with God.

THE GREEK WORDS

There is a large family of Greek words that can be translated "condemned." However, the basic word is *krino,* which means "to judge," or "to decide." There are a number of related words. The noun *krima* is usually rendered "condemnation" and means "to give judgment against," and thus "to condemn."

Another Greek word is *kataginosko,* and it means "to make a negative moral assessment," and thus "to blame."

Another Greek word is *katadikazo,* and it means "to pass judgment on."

Originally, krino and its associate words indicated simply an "assessment." A person examined a matter and then came to a conclusion about it.

By New Testament times, these words had become a part of the legal terminology used to speak of bringing charges, of judging, and of passing judgment. When used of God, krima (judgment), is understood as "condemnation," for one judged by God is already condemned.

DIVINE CONDEMNATION IN THE NEW TESTAMENT

The New Testament reminds us that Jesus did not enter our world to condemn us. He came because humanity was already condemned (Jn. 3:17-18; Rom. 5:15-16). Those who fail to respond to God's Word are in a state of condemnation already (Jn. 3:36; 12:48).

Jesus came to save the world. His success is reflected in assertions such as this: *"There is therefore now no condemnation to them which are in Christ Jesus, who walk not after the flesh, but after the Spirit"* (Rom. 8:1).

Because of Jesus, God's attitude toward believers is not one of condemnation. What God still condemns is the sin and sinners and those who walk after the flesh (Rom. 8:1, 3). We who respond to the gospel message in faith have the assurance that no one can successfully charge us. Jesus *"at the right hand of God"* also makes intercession for us (Rom. 8:34).

CONDEMNING OURSELVES AND OTHERS

Those who remain outside the circle of God's grace by their refusal to respond to the gospel (Jn. 3:18; 5:24) stand condemned; they are under judgment for their sinful actions (Mat. 12:41-42; Jn. 5:29; 12:48). However, we who have trusted Christ have passed beyond condemnation (Rom. 8:1).

God views us as being in His Son, and no charge can be lodged against us. Yet, two important truths are taught in the Scriptures about believers and condemnation. First, we are to be careful to do what is right so that our consciences will not condemn us for actions we believe are wrong (Rom. 14:22; I Jn. 3:20-21). Second, we are not to condemn fellow believers (Rom. 14:3).

Theologically, condemnation can be avoided only by trusting in Jesus and what He did for us at the Cross. He bears our sin and thus removes us from the position of prisoners before the bar of divine justice. Spiritually, we are to recognize the freedom from condemnation that Jesus brings us and learn to live as forgiven men and women.

Released from this burden ourselves, we are to bring the gospel to others so that they may be freed as well.

IT IS CHRIST WHO DIED

The heading refers to the price—the great, overwhelming, and absolutely paid price—that guarantees our salvation. In other words, when one condemns a fellow believer, one is condemning Christ, the price He paid, and the victory He won. In effect, one is saying that the price is not enough, insufficient, or is inadequate, for to condemn the believer is to condemn the price.

PENANCE AND PUNISHMENT

Who would be so foolish as to dare to do such a thing?

Of course Satan would do such a thing, even as we have already said; however, for believers to do such a thing proclaims to all that they have left grace and entered into the flesh or law. In other words, they are saying that the believer simply having faith in Christ and what He did at Calvary is not enough for his sins, but other penalties must be added as well. Whether such people say so or not, they are actually advocating the Catholic doctrine of penance.

To do penance is to carry out some task, whatever it may be, which is then supposed to pay for the sin. In fact, the major Pentecostal denominations engage in this foolishness, at least with their preachers. If something is done that is wrong, these preachers are forced to get out of the ministry for two years, or some such period of time, and sometimes forced to move to another city, etc. Also, they are demanded to enter into regular sessions with a psychologist and cannot be accepted again until they are signed off by a psychologist.

While they may personally deny that such is penance, but rather punishment, still it all amounts to the same. In the first place, no believer has the right, irrespective of who he may be, to condemn or to punish another believer. If that believer has done something wrong and refuses to cease the activity, whatever it might be, fellowship is to be withdrawn, but that is as far as it should go. The Lord has plainly said, *"Vengeance (punishment) is Mine; I will repay, says the Lord"* (Rom. 12:19).

James asks, *"Who are you who judges another?"* In other words, he is saying, "Who do you think you are, thinking you are qualified to judge someone else?" (James 4:12).

He then went on to say that the Lord was the only one who was qualified to judge.

A PERSONAL EXPERIENCE

I was speaking to a preacher the other day, and he mentioned to me that a certain Pentecostal denomination did thus and so to their preachers if somebody did something that was wrong. In other words, repentance and ceasing of the activity was not enough; they had to be punished for it.

I said to him, "Well, that means that what Jesus did at the Cross was not enough, and we have to add something to it."

He stood there for a moment saying nothing, and then wheeled around, looked at me for a few moments, and said, "I've never thought of that, but you are right."

Once again, it is a condemnation of the price that Jesus paid at the Cross, which is enough. To insinuate that more is needed is a great insult to the plan of God.

In the first place, there is no human being in the world that is saved and Spirit-filled, in whatever place and position they may occupy, who is worthy to condemn or to punish another. Anyone who thinks he is, is saying more about himself than God is saying. As well, and which we've already stated, it is an insult to the price that our Lord has already paid.

Some may ask, "Don't we have to show the world that we are hard on sin?" What if God did the same thing? What if every time we failed in some way, He took the position that He had to beat up on us severely to show the world how hard He is on sin?

The truth is that the Lord showed how hard He is on sin by giving His only Son to die on the Cross of Calvary. That showed what He thought of sin.

YES RATHER, WHO IS RISEN AGAIN

The resurrection of Christ refers to the ratification of that which He purchased for sinners in His death. The resurrection ratified the fact that Jesus was the perfect sacrifice and that God accepted it as such. However, it must ever be understood that the Cross did not depend on the resurrection; the resurrection depended on the Cross. If the sacrifice was accepted, and it definitely was, then the resurrection was a guaranteed fact.

If God has accepted the sacrifice of His only Son, and has proven it by raising Him from the dead, which He did, then who are we, or anyone else for that matter, to question such by condemning those who have placed their trust and faith in Him?

These are bold statements, and every believer should readily and soberly understand what is being said, and adhere to it very cautiously.

... WHO IS EVEN AT THE RIGHT HAND OF GOD ...

The heading refers to the exaltation of Christ.

When He ascended, He was then given His rightful place at the throne of God. It is at His Father's right hand. This speaks of power and authority. Actually, Jesus said after His resurrection, *"All power is given unto Me in heaven and in earth"* (Mat. 28:18).

Our faith should rest on Christ's death, but to that must be joined His resurrection and dominion, for without such His death was to no avail. He as the last Adam purchased back for us what the first Adam lost. As well, we must ever understand that at this very moment He is exalted at the right hand of God and is there for a divine purpose.

... WHO ALSO MAKES INTERCESSION FOR US

The heading tells us what that purpose is.

The intercession He makes is different than the intercession made by the Holy Spirit for us, as we have previously stated. The latter is that of help, while the former is that of guaranteeing our redemption and the forgiveness, cleansing, and washing of all sin from our lives. His intercession guarantees not only what He has already done respecting our salvation, but guarantees any future sin to be washed and cleansed, as well, at least upon repentance and confession (I Jn. 1:9).

UNDERSTANDING THE INTERCESSION OF JESUS ON OUR BEHALF

Most believers think their understanding of the intercession provided for us by Christ is correct, that is, if they have thought of it at all. With some that certainly may be true, but with the majority I fear their understanding is inadequate.

Actually, when a believer fails and seeks forgiveness, Jesus does not turn to the Father and ask Him to forgive us of whatever infraction that may have been committed. He doesn't have to do that. His very presence at the throne of God, meaning that He has been accepted, meaning that His sacrifice at Calvary's Cross has been accepted, guarantees that forgiveness, and restoration will instantly be granted. Calvary did it all, and for us to think that something must be added, at the same time says that Calvary didn't pay it all. The mere presence of Christ guarantees that His sacrifice was accepted, and guarantees the intercession on our behalf. In a sense, to properly understand His intercession on our behalf, we have to understand it in the same context as that of His death and resurrection. Actually, even as Paul here now makes the case, it is placed in that category, consequently linked together.

THE PSALMS

Most would hardly understand the psalms as the explanation of this extremely important subject of intercession, but they are. In some Bibles, the words "Messianic psalm" are listed above a psalm, which means that particular psalm refers to Jesus in some way—His life or His mission. By these identification characteristics, it is being said that only these psalms apply to Jesus, while the others apply to other things. But the truth is that all of the psalms, with some few exceptions, refer to Jesus Christ in some way.

WHAT THE PSALMS TELL US

The book of Psalms is a volume of prophecy, and its principle predictions concern the perfection, sufferings, and succeeding glories of the Messiah. With God having been dishonored by human unbelief and disobedience, it was necessary that a man should be born who would perfectly love, trust, and serve Him. He would be the true Adam, the true Noah, the true Abraham, the true Moses, the true David, and, actually, the true Israel.

God's moral glory demanded that sin should be judged, and that sinner's should repent, confess, and forsake sin, and worship and obey Him. Being God, His nature required perfection in these emotions of the heart and will.

Such perfection was impossible to fallen man, and it was equally out of his power to provide a sacrifice that would remove his guilt and restore His relationship with God.

The psalms reveal Christ as satisfying, in these relationships, all of the divine requirements. In a sense, He declares Himself in these psalms to be the sinner, even though He never sinned. He expresses to God the abhorrence of sin, accomplished by the repentance and sorrow that man ought to feel and express, but will not and cannot. Similarly, the faith, love, obedience, and worship that man fails to give, He renders perfectly. It is all for us and all on our behalf.

AS THE HIGH PRIEST OF HIS PEOPLE

Thus as the High Priest of His people, Christ, the true advocate, charges Himself with the guilt of our sins. He declares them to be His own, even though He never sinned, not even one single time. He confesses them, repents of them, and, at the same time, He declares His own sinlessness. Then He atones for them.

Actually, Psalm 51 provides the prayer of David for forgiveness, and even more perfectly the intercessory prayer prayed by Christ at the outset, which will stand through the ages. This psalm addresses three things:

1. David and his crying to God for mercy and grace respecting his terrible sin against Bathsheba and her husband Uriah.

2. In a sense it also is the prayer that Israel will pray when she comes to the very edge of total annihilation at the hands of the Antichrist in the battle of Armageddon. God will answer that prayer, which will culminate in the second coming of our Lord. Then the Antichrist (and the world, for that matter) is going to find out exactly who Jesus Christ really is.

3. Above all, it is the great prayer of intercession made by Christ on behalf of sinners. In fact, it is going on even today and will go on until the conclusion of the kingdom age when there will be no need for more intercession, for there will be no more sin.

Thus, those psalms in which the speaker declares his sinfulness (again, after a fashion, all on our behalf) and, at the same time, His sinlessness—when it's recognized who the speaker is—they become clear to comprehend.

This is the manner of the intercession of our Lord.

WHAT MOST THINK

As stated, if most believers think about it at all, they visualize Jesus as turning to the Father and asking Him to forgive them of whatever needs to be forgiven. The Father hears Him and does what He requests. However, that is not the way it happens.

When Jesus took our place at Calvary, He actually became a sin offering (Isa. 53:10). As a result, punishment was loaded on Him, with sin's demands met, which was death, and the curse of the law was then satisfied. Upon faith, the believing sinner is literally in Him when He died, at least in the mind of God (Rom. 6:3-4; 8:1). The same holds for His burial and resurrection. Of course, all of this is spiritual, with none of it being physical, except on the part of Christ. If one is to notice, it continues in the exultation, even as Paul speaks here concerning Jesus at the right hand of God. Paul said, *"And has raised us up together, and made us sit together in heavenly places in Christ Jesus"* (Eph. 2:6). So, as Christ is seated at the right hand of the Father, we are in effect seated with Him and in Him.

However, it does not stop there, but continues in the same manner respecting the failures and sins of believers. Jesus takes these failures and sins, makes them His own, even though He has never sinned, and seeks for forgiveness, even though He never failed.

As stated, it is all done in the prayer of David respecting Psalm 51. Because He has never failed, and thereby was the perfect sacrifice, forgiveness is always automatic, which extends to the believer because we are in Him.

So, His intercession for us is of far grander magnitude than first thought. It is not merely a request for others, even as important and wonderful as that would be, but in reality it is the taking of our place, even as He has always taken our place.

THE WONDER OF IT ALL

When one thinks of this, it is beyond comprehension. It amazes us even as it should amaze us. What a mighty God we serve, and what a wonderful Christ who has saved us.

God's requirements must be satisfied in order that His righteousness not be abrogated. That is not a matter of stubbornness, but rather of necessity. God wants to approach us and us to approach Him, but in a sinful condition on our part, such could not be done. Therefore, He made it possible by becoming man—*the* Man Christ Jesus. In so doing, He served as the representative man, and for all who will believe, the Saviour of all the ages.

When one thinks of what Paul is saying here, it humbles one, or certainly should. Why He would love us in this fashion I think we will never know. Yet we know He does. Even at this very moment, as I dictate these words, He is making intercession for us. The moment you read them, whatever time of day that it is, He will be faithful in continuing this all-important task until one day when we stand before Him, ever precious in His sight.

There are many examples in the psalms of His personal intercession. As He does this (even declaring Himself a sinner) all on our behalf and in our place (even though He has never sinned), because of a lack of understanding of true intercession on the part of many, they do not recognize these psalms as being of Christ, even as all the others. For instance, of all the many psalms that could be chosen, Psalm 51 is perhaps the greatest example.

It is the plea of David, but also, and of far greater significance, it is the prayer of intercession of the Son of David.

———————⊱·✕·⊰———————

Joys are flowing like a river,
Since the Comforter has come;
He abides with us forever,
Makes the trusting heart His home.

Bringing life and health and gladness,
All around this heavenly Guest,
Banished unbelief and sadness,
Changed our weariness to rest.

Like the rain that falls from heaven,
Like the sunlight from the sky,
So the Holy Ghost is given,
Coming on us from on high.

See, a fruitful field is growing,
Blessed fruit of righteousness;
And the streams of life are flowing
In the lonely wilderness.

What a wonderful salvation,
Where we always see His face!
What a perfect habitation,
What a quiet resting place!

Blessed quietness, holy quietness
What assurance in my soul!
On the stormy sea He speaks peace to me,
How the billows cease to roll!

HOW THE HOLY SPIRIT WORKS

THE LOVE OF CHRIST

THE LOVE OF CHRIST

"WHO SHALL SEPARATE US from the love of Christ? Shall tribulation, or distress, or persecution, or famine, or nakedness, or peril, or sword?" (Rom. 8:35).

WHO SHALL SEPARATE US
FROM THE LOVE OF CHRIST?

As long as the church preaches the Cross, it is preaching the gospel. If not, what it is preaching is of little or no consequence.

If one is to notice, the heading speaks of the love of Christ for the believer instead of the believer's love for Christ.

In Romans 8:35–39 some have attempted to promote the unscriptural doctrine of unconditional eternal security, to which we have briefly touched on. But due to the great significance of this subject, please allow the repetition.

This doctrine teaches that after one is truly saved, one cannot be lost, irrespective of what he may do, how deep he may go into sin and remain there, or even how much he denies Christ and loses his faith. Of course, this doctrine is not scriptural for many and varied reasons, but the main reason is that it abrogates all personal responsibility, as well as violates the free moral agency of man. In effect, as we have already stated, it is another form of the erroneous doctrine of predestination to be saved or lost, and there is nothing anyone can do to change that situation.

We believe and teach conditional eternal security—conditional on the premise that our faith remain in Christ and what He has done for us at the Cross. Ceasing to believe that is the only thing that will take one out of the bonds of salvation. Sin will not do it; if it did, there would be no one saved. It is faith in Christ and what He did at the Cross that got us in, and it is faith in Christ and the Cross that keeps us in.

A denial of His sacrificial offering of Himself on Calvary's Cross will revert one back to a lost state (Heb. 6:1-6; 10:28-31).

GOD WILL NOT PROTECT US FROM OURSELVES

While it is true that God protects the believer (as is recorded here) from all outside adversity, that is at least as it refers to one's salvation, there is nothing in these passages which says that God protects the believer from himself. In other words, the believer still retains the power of choice, and it is that choice that decides his eternal destiny. No, it is not that man's choice is greater than God. Such thinking is silly. However, God has given man the privilege of choice, and, in effect, the love spoken of here has to be by choice, or it simply cannot be love, whether it is on the part of God or man.

In other words, the very nature of one's living for God has to be on the principle of choice. It is the same with a husband and wife—one cannot force the other to love; it must be one's own prerogative. It is the same with God. We must freely love Him, or else it is not love.

In fact, this is the manner in which God made man in the very beginning. Had He wanted some type of human computer, He would have easily made man without a will. However, to obtain that which He desired, which is that man would freely love Him, man had to be given the power of choice.

SHALL TRIBULATION, OR DISTRESS, OR PERSECUTION, OR FAMINE, OR NAKEDNESS, OR PERIL, OR SWORD?

The heading presents the foe's armory as containing seven weapons—the whole of his resources:

- Tribulation
- Distress
- Persecution
- Famine
- Nakedness
- Peril
- Sword

However these weapons may disfigure, deform, degrade, or denigrate the believer, yet Christ will still love and prize him. For instance, Joseph was just as dear to that love when lying in the dungeon as when seated on the throne. It is possible to separate from human love, but not from Christ's love. For instance, a man may love his betrothed very deeply, but if by the power of an enemy her beauty and her character were destroyed, it is possible that his love for her would die; but that's not how God is toward those who are His.

This text speaks and pertains to the love of Christ for the believer; however, on the other side of the coin, these things are allowed by God as detrimental as they may seem on the surface, to deepen our love for God rather than the opposite. And so it does.

Satan uses these weapons to try to separate us from the love of Christ, not so much regarding the Lord loving us, for the enemy knows that is impossible. However, he does have the mistaken idea that these foes will weaken our love for God. There is a reason for that.

JOB

Satan claimed that Job loved God not because of who God is, but for what God had done for Job (Job 1). Actually, that is the entire contention of Satan against God.

He claimed then that men loved God because of the wonderful things the Lord did for them, and he continues to do the same presently. He refuses to admit that men love God simply because of who He is. In other words, we will love Him irrespective of what He does for us in the material and physical sense. Whether it is poverty or riches, we will love Him. Whether it is health or sickness, we will love Him. That and that alone is true Christianity.

Satan refuses to acknowledge that, which actually is the bedrock of serving God. In other words, we serve Him for who He is rather than for the things He gives us.

ONE REASON THAT THE MODERN GREED GOSPEL IS SO EVIL

This so-called gospel, which in reality is another gospel, makes money the priority. In other words, and irrespective as to how much it is denied, money and money alone is that gospel. Jesus Christ and what He did at Calvary plus the entirety of the plan of salvation to redeem humanity from sin's terrible bondage is cheapened to mere things. Hence, Jesus said, *"Take heed, and beware of covetousness: For a man's life consists not in the abundance of the things which he possesses"* (Lk. 12:15).

While God most definitely does bless people, and abundantly we might quickly add, as well as financially, still this is not the main thrust of the gospel, and in fact never has been. It plays right into Satan's hands with his age-old contention that no one truly loves God. Any supposed love, he says, is merely a ploy to get things. So the preachers who claim this as their message are not preaching the gospel and are not winning people to Christ. They are actually playing into the hands of the Evil One.

If we forget the true purpose for which Jesus came, which is to redeem man from sin, then we have totally abrogated all that He did at Calvary. Then as stated, we are preaching *"another gospel"* (II Cor. 11:3–4).

THE ENTIRETY OF THE SO-CALLED
CONFESSION MESSAGE

This false message that is prominent today and has been prominent for several decades, claims that if the believer has enough faith and his confession is proper, he can void all of these tribulations, distresses, etc. (This fits right in with the greed message, and in fact, is the greed message.) But the entirety of the tenor of the Bible presents the very opposite: the believer is not exempt from those things.

The people in the world who are giving Satan great problems are the true believers—those who believe in Christ and what He did for us at the Cross. Consequently, Satan will use every means at his disposal to attempt to stop the child of God, as should be obvious. In fact, the believer is at war and will be at war with the Evil One, at least regarding his faith, until the trump of God sounds (II Cor. 10:3-5).

However, if one will study church history, one will find that great opposition and persecution by the powers of darkness, in whatever manner these came even to the giving of one's life, have never weakened or hurt the true church of the living God. For all who were snatched from its ranks, several others took their place, even knowing that it could mean their lives, as well. So, persecution has really never hurt the church—it actually only strengthened the church, i.e., the individual believer. To be frank, this is one of the very reasons that persecution is allowed by the Lord. That which weakens, hinders, and stunts the spiritual growth and turns aside the believer is the opposite message with which we have been regaled for the last several decades—the false greed message.

LEAVEN

I realize that some readers may think I am overly hard on this particular subject; however, if that be the case, it is not preachers, per se, to whom I address these remarks, but rather the message itself. It is the lie to which I am opposed and not the people themselves. Yet I realize that it is very difficult to separate the man and his message, perhaps impossible. Consequently, it is incumbent upon the preacher of the gospel not to allow his heart to be adversely affected by the propagators of this false message, but to stay focused on the true task at hand—the Evil One who is behind all of this, Satan himself.

Let not the believer think that Satan doesn't know what he is doing. In fact, his greatest weapon is to make his message sound as near to the true message as possible. So near, in fact, that it takes one truly close to God to actually see the difference. He loads up his lie with truth, which makes it very plausible, but it is the leaven that is hidden in the truth that must be exposed, which causes so much danger respecting the believer (I Cor. 5:6). Irrespective as to how small the amount of leaven may be at the beginning, if it is not removed, it will ultimately take over the whole, until there is nothing left but leaven. That is the very nature of leaven. That is Satan's purpose, and he is very good at what he does—mixing error with truth. As someone has well said, "All error rides into the church on the back of truth."

AS IT IS WRITTEN, FOR YOUR SAKE
WE ARE KILLED ALL THE DAY LONG

"As it is written, for Your sake we are killed all the day long; we are accounted as sheep for the slaughter" (Rom. 8:36).

If the Cross is removed from the gospel, there is no gospel left. The Cross of Christ is not something that happened just 2,000 years ago, but in reality was begun before the foundation of the world (I Pet. 1:18-20).

The heading is taken from Psalm 44:22. If one carefully reads that particular psalm, it speaks of God who had done great things for His people, but then seemingly withdrew His hand of help and protection and allowed His people to be overcome. However, verses 20 and 21 tell us why.

Israel had strayed, and *"God* (would) *search this out? For He knows the secrets of the heart"* (Ps. 44:22).

The Lord allows tribulation for two purposes:

1. To expose the leaven in our lives.
2. To draw us nearer to God. It is sad that believers need such chastisement, but often we do.

WE ARE ACCOUNTED AS SHEEP
FOR THE SLAUGHTER

The heading proclaims a great truth that we should learn.

When the believing sinner comes to Christ, his life ceases to be his own, and it becomes the property and possession of our Lord. Consequently, at that moment, we give up our lives, which is exactly what Jesus told us to do. He said, *"For whosoever will save his life shall lose it: And whosoever will lose his life for My sake shall find it"* (Mat. 16:25).

One might ask how this statement by Christ could be so. If we understand the following, perhaps we can understand it better.

The Lord doesn't look at time factors as we do, but He looks at eternity. If you save your life in this particular life, which means you'll lose it, what have you profited? However, if you lose your life for the cause of Christ, you have saved it for all eternity, and there is nothing that can compare eternity with our present lifespan.

MODERN BELIEVERS

One of the great problems of modern believers is that sometimes we are attempting (erroneously, I might add) to build a paradise out of this present life, which makes us not too desirous of the one to come. That's exactly what is happening presently. It's the "me" and "now" instead of the "Thou" and "then." If one is to notice the attitude of the early church, their hearts were on things above. I am afraid that presently too many of us have our hearts on things below. Once again, and even though I am overly repetitive, the modern greed gospel fits perfectly into that scheme.

While the believer has a great work at this present time to do, and while that work is of extreme importance, still, the believer must ever know and realize that the sons of God have not yet been manifested. That will happen only when Jesus comes.

Please allow me to ask this question: How many believers (for whatever reason) truly want Jesus to come at this present time? Some few do, while most know nothing about His coming, or else they have been erroneously taught, thinking that His coming depends on them. Nothing could be crasser, even the height of prideful absurdity. Such is the modern kingdom message.

NO, IN ALL THESE THINGS WE ARE MORE THAN CONQUERORS

"No, in all these things we are more than conquerors through Him who loved us" (Rom. 8:37).

Every soul saved and every prayer answered is because of Jesus and what He did for us at the Cross.

The heading means that such has never stopped the true church of God, and such will never be successful in that effort.

In the Greek, the phrase, *"More than conquerors,"* is *hupernikao,* and means "to conquer, to carry off the victory, to come off victorious." However, the Greek word *huper* attached to *nikao,* means "above," thus: "to come off more than victorious, to gain a surprising victory." It is a holy arrogance of victory in the might of Christ.

Perhaps it is a mistake to define in what the *"more"* consists of. If we do, the answer must be sought on the line indicated in the note, *"For Your sake we are killed all the day long."* These trials not only do not cut us off from Christ's love, they actually give us more intimate and thrilling experience of it.

THROUGH HIM WHO LOVED US

The phrase, *"Through Him who loved us,"* means that He allowed these things to come to pass, not to destroy us, but rather the very opposite. It is because of His love, which some have called tough love, that He allows adversities.

Such draws the believer closer to God for the simple reason that we know our only hope is in Christ. As well, these great victories won by the child of God, despite the worst of adversities, portray to all of heaven, as well as the darkened host of Satan, that God's people do not serve Him for things, but rather because they love Him. In other words, we are willing to lay down our lives for His sake.

The "conquering" carries the idea, not so much of deliverance from these things, but rather that we did not allow these adversities to sully our testimony, but to sharpen our testimony.

In other words, these who have gone through such trials (and many have) did not do so because of a lack of faith, but rather because of their great faith. Actually, it was meant to strengthen their faith, which it did.

FOR I AM PERSUADED

"For I am persuaded, that neither death, nor life, nor angels, nor principalities, nor powers, nor things present, nor things to come, nor height, nor depth, nor any other creature, shall be able to separate us from the love of God, which is in Christ Jesus our Lord" (Rom. 8:38-39).

It was to Paul that the great word of the Cross was given, and he gave it to us in his 14 epistles.

Ninety percent of what he gave us has to do with the Cross of Christ, not with salvation, as important as that is, but rather with our sanctification. Yet most modern preachers while having a modicum of knowledge respecting the Cross concerning salvation have none at all as it regards sanctification. The heading over the verse comes from the heart of the apostle, meaning that he had faced the things of which he now speaks.

There are probably few people in history, if any, who have suffered as Paul suffered in order to take the gospel of Jesus Christ to a hurting world, which means to establish the church, which he did.

While the victory of his heart, even according to this verbiage was overflowing with strength and power, with Satan making no headway there, still the Evil One fought the apostle on every hand with beatings, stonings, shipwreck, and about everything that one could possibly think. So when he says, *"I am persuaded,"* it refers to something, or rather someone, who has stood the test, namely himself.

THAT NEITHER DEATH

The heading means that Jesus has pulled the teeth of that monster. The true believer no longer fears death, with untold numbers down through history having willingly laid down their lives for the cause of Christ. In fact, not long after the writing of the book of Acts, Rome turned ugly toward the church, with the floors of its arenas turning red with the spilled blood of those who died for Jesus.

The world of that day other than Christendom was plagued with a myriad of gods. In other words, there were all types of gods worshipped by all types of people.

Consequently, the Roman senate voted that their Caesar, whoever he might be, would be declared as deity or god. Most of the Caesars, realizing their humanity and consequent frailty, refused to have such a title attached to their names, but Nero demanded to be called "god." Consequently, untold thousands died by wild animals and Roman spears simply because they would not say, "Caesar is Lord." Their cry, even unto death, was, "Jesus is Lord!"

What a testimony!

APOSTASY OF THE CHURCH

As well, down through the Dark Ages, which were brought on by a forsaking of the gospel, the Church itself turned ugly. It forsook Christ, gradually evolved into what became known as the Catholic Church, and attempted to bring about the kingdom of God by force. As a result, untold thousands, with some even claiming millions, died for the cause of Christ simply because they refused allegiance to the Catholic Church and the pope. It was called the Dark Ages for a reason.

So, the great freedoms we presently have did not come cheaply. They were paid for with blood, and not only on the field of battle but even more so in the spirit world.

NOR LIFE

The phrase *"nor life"* refers to the vicissitudes or diffi-culties of life which come to the believer, even as Paul has here enumerated.

Someone has said, and perhaps rightly so, that at times it is harder to live for God than it is to die for Him.

NOR ANGELS

The phrase, *"nor angels,"* refers to fallen angels, who threw in their lot with Lucifer, himself an Angel, when he rebelled against God in the ages of the past (Isa. 14; Ezek. 28).

These fallen angels are powerful beings, helping Satan orchestrate and manage his kingdom of darkness. Consequently, they are very much involved in the opposition against the child of God, helping to carry out these evil schemes. We are here assured, however, that if we will cling to Jesus, their power is foiled irrespective as to what they may attempt.

NOR PRINCIPALITIES

The phrase *"nor principalities,"* refers to the satanic powers of Ephesians 2:2 and 6:12.

These are fallen angels of greater power than normal, and are, in fact, in charge of certain areas of the world. They are chief rulers of the highest rank and order in Satan's kingdom (Col. 2:10).

NOR POWERS

The phrase *"nor powers,"* again refers to fallen angels who derive their power from and execute the will of the chief rulers, i.e., chief angels.

If one is to notice, this speaks of the world being divided into areas, with powerful fallen angels in charge of certain sections, with other angels under them carrying out instructions, all under the chief fallen angel—Satan himself. This is evident in Daniel 10. The powerful fallen angels which were being fought by Gabriel and Michael—the most powerful Angels in God's kingdom—concerned spiritual authority in the world. (For more information on this very important subject, please see our *Jimmy Swaggart Bible Commentary: Daniel.*)

NOR THINGS PRESENT

The phrase *"nor things present,"* refers to present trials engineered by these *"principalities and powers."* The believer must understand that what we are up against in the spirit world is so far beyond our particular resources, that if we try to oppose these things in the wrong way, defeat will be our lot.

If we do this God's way, which is the way of the Holy Spirit, which is the way of the Cross, we will find victory. Otherwise, we won't.

Unfortunately, the modern church knows almost nothing about spiritual warfare. They are trying to combat these forces of darkness with humanistic psychology, with the power of positive thinking, or any other number of concoctions devised by men. It won't work, not even momentarily. Unfortunately, the Holy Spirit is presently preached in so few churches that most believers don't have the foggiest idea as to the great part that He plays, or at least desires to play in our everyday journey with the Lord. Consequently, wreckage is the lot of most believers.

NOR THINGS TO COME

The heading refers to the plans being made at this very moment against the kingdom of God by these fallen beings, which will materialize in the not too distant future. However, we need not fear, knowing that Jesus has defeated all of these powers of darkness. At least, I should quickly say, we need not fear if we do these things God's way, and I say it again: It is the way of the Cross.

Satan and all of his cohorts of darkness were defeated at the Cross (Col. 2:10-15). This is the reason that Satan hates the Cross. This is the reason that he tries his best to stop the preaching of the Cross. It is because it is the place of his total and complete defeat.

NOR HEIGHT, NOR DEPTH

The phrase *"nor height, nor depth,"* refers to Satan as the *"prince of the powers of the air,"* and to the horrors of hell itself (Eph. 2:2).

"Height, nor depth," also refers to the severity of Satan's planned attack against the child of God. It will fail, as fail it must, that is if our faith is conclusively in Christ and Him crucified, which then guarantees the help of the Holy Spirit. The Holy Spirit is God, and as we are no match for the powers of Satan within ourselves, likewise neither Satan nor any of his cohorts of darkness are a match for the Holy Spirit.

NOR ANY OTHER CREATURE

The heading is not meant to insinuate that there are other spheres of operation that can oppose the child of God, other than Satan, his fallen angels, and demon spirits, but is meant to cover any and all things that may conceivably oppose the believer. In other words, the Holy Spirit through the apostle is saying that there is absolutely nothing that Satan can originate or institute against the believer that will be successful. That is true, if the believer will cling tenaciously to Christ and what He did for us at the Cross. Always remember the Cross of Christ is the place of Satan's total defeat, and that's why he hates it so much.

SHALL BE ABLE TO SEPARATE
US FROM THE LOVE OF GOD

The believer must understand that while God at times may be disappointed in us, He never withdraws His love. That we must understand.

Please read the following very carefully: If you as a believer fail the Lord in any way; if you sin—even a sin that is terrible one might say—don't run from the Lord, but rather run to the Lord. I know that fear at times fills our hearts when we fail the Lord, but please understand that the Lord has never been anything but gracious and kind to all of His children. If we will go to Him in humility and with love and grace, acknowledging our wrongdoing, He will respond accordingly, of that we can be certain.

WHICH IS IN CHRIST JESUS OUR LORD

The heading refers to everything we have, everything we have been given, and every privilege and blessing that has come our way. This includes our salvation, our baptism with the Holy Spirit, our eternal life, our redemption in totality, in fact, all. Of course, He means all being in, through, of, and by the Lord Jesus Christ. He is the manifestation of the Father, and in Him are all things. He is life, salvation, grace, mercy, compassion, and resurrection. He is our Saviour today and will be to all who will. However, if He is presently rejected as Saviour, men will find that they will have to face Him tomorrow as judge, but face Him they will. It's either the Cross or the great white throne judgment; we must not forget that.

JESUS AND HIS PEOPLE

His people love Him and believe in the fidelity of His love for us. Trials only assure the hearts of those who know

His love, and that nothing can separate them from it. Believers know that being called, justified, and glorified leaves no link wanting in the golden chain that binds us to His heart.

That chain begins in the immeasurable past and reaches into the immeasurable future. It stretches from one eternity to the other, one might say. Love and purpose planned that they should have the one and same portion with Himself. This faith makes us more than conquerors over *"all these things,"* i.e., these trials. Joseph, Daniel, Simon Peter, and Paul, etc., are examples.

THE ENEMY OF OUR SOULS

Let the enemy search death and life and the present and the future. Let him mount to the greatest heights or descend to the lowest depths. Let him turn to all created things and to men, Angels, and demons. He will fail to find any power that can separate the redeemed from the love of God that is in Christ Jesus our Lord.

A PERSONAL NOTE

The Lord saved me when I was 8 years of age and baptized me with the Holy Spirit a few weeks later. When I was 9 years old, I knew that I would be an evangelist, and I knew that this ministry would be worldwide. I didn't understand how, but I knew it would be.

When I was about 10 years old, I had an experience that was but a portent of that which was to come. The Lord showed me something in a dream. I dreamed I was standing out in front of our house in the little town in which I was born and raised—Ferriday, Louisiana. I looked to my right, and I saw a globe of this planet that was suspended in space, possibly about 10 or 15 feet from me. The globe was slowly turning, and I could see it was a globe of this planet, and it was about the size of a basketball. It seemed to be suspended in space, but as I stated, slowly turning.

All of a sudden, a figure was standing beside it, looking intently at it. I instantly recognized this figure to be Satan. Strangely enough, there was no fear in my heart, as I observed what was taking place.

After staring at the globe for a short period of time, he then turned and looked at me and said, "You will not do it; I will stop you."

He turned back and looked at the globe again, and then turned back to me, saying the same identical thing all over again: "You will not do it; I will stop you."

Satan meant what he said and set out almost from that moment to carry out his threats.

For me to enumerate all of these efforts by the Evil One would be pointless at this particular time. All believers suffer opposition from the powers of darkness; however I share the sentiments of the great preacher E.M. Bounds, who said, "Those who are a great threat to Satan feel the power of his opposition keenly."

I may not have his exact words, but that is close to his statement, and it is ever so true.

THE ATTITUDE OF THE BELIEVER

No, I am not blaming wrongdoing or failure on Satan for the simple reason that all wrongdoing is the fault of the individual, irrespective of the circumstances. However, for anyone to think that the matter is simple, that person is either hypocritical, or else he has never faced the powers of darkness simply because he is doing very little, if anything, for the Lord Jesus Christ.

Some time ago, I read a message by a preacher who lived and ministered in the 1700s. In his message he made a statement that I think is well worth repeating:

When one hears something negative about a fellow believer, one should treat it as gossip, which means to ignore it, and above all to never repeat such slander, because slander is what it is. If one feels one has firsthand knowledge of the circumstances, still, are you sure that you know and understand the degree of spiritual warfare involved? If you had been placed in the same circumstances, would you have done any better or even as well?

As I close this book, I want to go back to Romans 8:2 and with great joy and thanksgiving say with the apostle Paul: *"For the law of the Spirit of life in Christ Jesus has made me free from the law of sin and death."*

We must never forget that all victory—and I mean all victory—is ever in Christ Jesus and what He has done for us at the Cross.

As someone has well said: "Satan says things about me, people say things about me, and God says things about me. It is only what God says that matters."

———⊃·◇◇·⊂———

I've seen the lightning flashing,
And heard the thunder roll,
I've felt sin's breakers dashing,
Trying to conquer my soul;
I've heard the voice of my Savior,
Telling me still to fight on,
He promised never to leave me,
Never to leave me alone.

No, never alone,
No, never alone,
He promised never to leave me,
Never to leave me alone;
No, never alone,
No, never alone,
He promised never to leave me,
Never to leave me alone.

ABOUT EVANGELIST JIMMY SWAGGART

The Rev. Jimmy Swaggart is a Pentecostal evangelist whose anointed preaching and teaching has drawn multitudes to the Cross of Christ since 1955.

As an author, he has written more than 50 books, commentaries, study guides, and The Expositor's Study Bible, which has sold more than 3.6 million copies.

As an award-winning musician and singer, Brother Swaggart has recorded more than 50 gospel albums and sold nearly 17 million recordings worldwide.

For more than six decades, Brother Swaggart has channeled his preaching and music ministry through multiple media venues including print, radio, television and the Internet.

In 2010, Jimmy Swaggart Ministries launched its own cable channel, SonLife Broadcasting Network, which airs 24 hours a day to a potential viewing audience of more than 2 billion people around the globe.

Brother Swaggart also pastors Family Worship Center in Baton Rouge, Louisiana, the church home and headquarters of Jimmy Swaggart Ministries.

Jimmy Swaggart Ministries materials can be found at **www.jsm.org**.

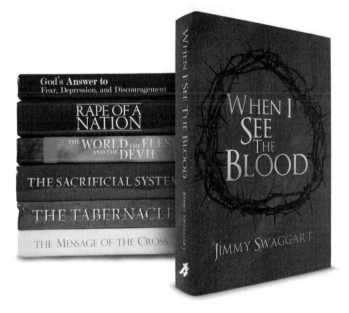